Gardening: The Rockwool Book

By George F. Van Patten

Van Patten Publishing, Portland, Oregon

Gardening: The Rockwool Book

By George F. Van Patten

Published by: **Van Patten Publishing**
4204 S. E. Ogden
Portland, OR 97206
U.S.A.

ISBN: 1-878823-00-0 $14.95 Softcover

Photos on pages 4, 5, 7, 10-12, 40, 41, 64-66, 81, 84, curtsey of **Agro Dynamics**, East Brunswick, New Jersey

Warning - Disclaimer

This book is written for the purpose of supplying gardening information to the public. It is sold with the agreement that it does not offer any guarantee of plant growth or well-being. Readers of this book are responsible for all plants cultivated. You are encouraged to read any and all information available about hydroponic gardening, rockwool and gardening in general to develop a complete background on the subjects so you can taylor this information to your individual needs. This book should be used as a general guide to gardening with rockwool and not the ultimate source.

The author and Van Patten Publishing have tried to the best of their ability to describe all of the most current methods to garden successfully using rockwool. However, there may be mistakes in the text that the author and publisher were unable to detect. This book contains current information up to the date of publication.

The publisher nor the author endorse any products or brand names that are mentioned or pictured in the text. Products are pictured or mentioned for illustration only.

Table of Contents

Chapter One

Rockwool

Rockwool is the biggest innovation in growing mediums since sterilized soil. This revolutionary new soilless medium consists of thin strand-like fibers made from rocks. Growing hydroponically without soil in rockwool is very productive and easy.

Mother Nature demonstrated rockwool to modern man on the islands of Hawaii as a volcanic production the mid 1800's. Volcanos B erupt tiny droplets of molten lava. The droplets of lava are sprayed high into the air. Strong tropical winds whip this magma into long, thin hair-like fibers. Known in Hawaii as Pele's hair", the god of volcanos', this natural fiber (rockwool) has been collected for centuries and used as a medium to cultivate orchids and other plants. By 1865, it was produced in the United States for insulation. In fact, the walls in your home may be packed full of rockwool. In Denmark, over 100 years later, rockwool was first developed commercially for horticulture. In 1985, horticultural rockwool, glass wool, growool, or mineral wool was introduced into the U.S. and Canada.

Like perlite, vermiculite and numerous other soilless mixes, rockwool was originally used by commercial growers. Later home gardeners discovered the numerous ways that it improves garden soil and in many cases replaces soil.

Organic growing mediums like peat, sawdust and soils are becoming more expensive to produce, they decompose and their water holding capacity changes. Inorganic mediums such as sand, graveland perlite do not hold as much solution as rockwool nor do they offer much buffering capacity. These attributes, coupled with the high cost of sterilization, prompted European growers to explore new alternatives.

Danish growers began growing hydroponically in rockwool in 1969 to overcome the ban on soilgrown nursery stock imposed by neighboring European countries. Now, essentially all cucumber crops in Denmark are grown in rockwool. Today, an estimated 50 percent of all Western European greenhouse vegetables are grown exclusively in rockwool. In Holland, land under cultivation in rockwool doubled from 2,500 acres in 1984 to 5,000 acres.

Rockwool caught on fast in Canada's progressive greenhouse industry. Greenhouse vegetable growers from Nova Scotia to British Columbia are using more rockwool every year.

Japan began producing horticultural rockwool in 1984. Since then, Japanese growers have started the switch to rockwool. Rockwool simply offers them the best value. One of the major uses the Japanese have found for rockwool is to propagate rice.

A strong cucumber crop in rockwool slabs.

Soil is difficult for American growers to abandon as we still have acres of fertile land available. Some growers, however, have tried using rockwool indoors with fantastic results. It's water holding capability promotes easy care, fast, and controlled growth which is ideal for cuttings and seedlings.

Rockwool is very different from soil. Soil is wonderful! My wife and I have large raised bed vegetable and flower gardens. The soil is totally organic. We love to play in the good earth outdoors. How do you describe the feeling of getting dirty,

A young pepper plant growing in a cube
placed on a slab.

tilling the soil, looking for earthworms cut worms, and slug tracks? The simple
pleasure of sowing seeds in rich organic soil and nurturing the sprouting
seedlings throughout life is very rewarding.

   A rockwool garden will not perform like a soil garden. Root crops, trees
and vines such as potatoes, horseradish, asparagus, fruit trees, kiwis and grapes
are better suited to soil.
   Popular rockwool crops are tomatoes, cucumbers, peepers, lettuce, roses,
freesias, and orchids just to name a few.
   Rockwool is a better value than other mediums and can last indefinitely
with care and sterilization. In fact, one-inch rockwool cubes retail for half the cost
of peat pellets. Plus the rockwool cubes are easier to transplant than peat
pellets, which require removal of the outer plastic mesh.
   The best rockwool garden will yield 10 to 20 percent more produce than
the best soil garden. This easy-to-achieve yield coupled with a few simple
cultivation techniques can make rockwool produce twice as much   as   soil.

Rockwool is very well suited for seedlings and cuttings, while larger slabs make attractive patio gardens.

Horticultural rockwool is produced from rock basalt and is usually a combination of rock, limestone and coke. The best horticultural rockwools are produced from volcanic basaltic rock (diabase). These rockwools have a mineral balance that is inert and will not react adversely with the nutrient solution. Some insulation-grade rockwool is produced from steel or copper slag, a waste by-product from smelting. These rockwools contain a high amount of metals, mainly copper and iron, that may react with the nutrient solution. The high quality horticultural rockwools have uniform fibers, even distribution of the binder and very little "shot" or slag (mineral pellets that have not been spun into fiber). This high quality rockwool weighs less than five pounds per cubic foot. Low quality, insulation-grade rockwool has more of this problem causing "shot" and weighs seven pounds or more per cubic foot.

Insulation grade rockwool compacts fairly easily. Although still porous and well draining, this compaction upsets the air-water ratio that is so important to all hydroponic growing. The other problem with the insulation grade is pH drift which is caused by substances that are released into the nutrient solution, primarily potassium hydroxide, which is used to raise the pH. This is a natural by-product of the weathering of basalt; potassium hydroxide causes the pH to continually drift up above seven to as high as ten in extreme cases. A high pH causes precipitates, primarily gypsum and locks out or makes unavailable many elements that the plants need from the nutrient solution.

Rockwool fibers naturally repel water because they are coated with a type of mineral oil. During manufacturing, the mineral oils are removed from high quality horticultural rockwool and replaced with mineral wetting agents when the rock is melted. Lower quality insulation grade rockwool does not remove the water repelling mineral oils; a chemical wetting agent (similar to liquid dish soap) that allows the naturally water repelling rockwool to hold water is added. The wetting agent washes out and must be added regularly. Some commercial fertilizers, such as EcoGrow, contain a wetting agent to counteract this loss.

NOTE: Uniform wetting is one of rockwool's most important qualities. It promotes even root growth, no dry or wet pockets and provides even drainage.

The rigid rock components are melted at temperatures between 1,500 and 3,000 degrees Fahrenheit. This molten solution is poured or sprayed over a spinning disk. As the molten solution flies off the disk, it elongates and cools to form hair-like fibers. The process is very similar to the way liquified sugar is poured on a spinning disk to make cotton candy. The molten sugar spins in the air and cools into long fibrous strands of cotton candy.

Rockwool spinning off the wheels in a manufacturing plant.

How Rockwool Is Made

A binder (phenol-based resin) is added to the product of these fibers of rockwool just after the spinning process. This plasticlike binder prevents potassium hydroxide and other elements from leaching into the nutrient solution. After the binder is added, the rockwool is compressed and cured into large uniform slabs, starter cubes or granular flock. The amount of pressure applied when forming the slabs dictates the density of the rockwool. The blocks are rigid and easy to handle. They may be cut into just about any size or shape. Granulated rockwool flock is easily placed into growing containers or used like vermiculite, perlite or peat moss as a soil additive.

The heat used to produce rockwool renders it sterile and safe for growing plants. The length and thickness of the rockwool fibers are regulated by the speed of the spinning disk, the consistency of the molten rock mix and the melt temperature. Different densities are made at this stage. The most consistent horticultural rockwool is made from four disks spinning toward one another. The fibers spin off the first disk and are caught by the second, then the third and the fourth disk. The end product of the fourth disk is most consistent, containing little shot.

The grain or the direction the fibers run in rockwool is important to water absorption. Fibers normally run horizontally in slabs. The horizontal grain allows the nutrient solution to drain slower from the slab allowing good lateral capillary movement and retaining even moisture. Roots spread out with the grain. Propagation and small cubes have vertical grain. The vertical grained cubes are perfect for the more rapid fast draining required by seedlings and clones, and roots grow downwards. The random orientation of the grain in rockwool flock or bulk rockwool promotes root growth in all directions.

Larger rockwool slabs do not necessarily bring a higher yield. But a larger chunk of rockwool makes a larger reservoir to hold nutrient solution and is more reliable. Six-inch slabs are as good as eight-inch slabs for crops that grow up to five or six months. Six-inch slabs are ideal for most hobby gardens, and more economical. I like 8-inch slabs for rectangular and square shaped gardens. The wider slab offers more ballast for larger plants, but if plants grow too tall, they still should be staked or tied up.

Even though rockwool will hold 10-14 times as much water as soil, it does not provide the buffering action available in soil. The pH or acid to alkaline balance of dry rockwool is about 7.8 to 8.0. A pH lowering agent is added to the water solution to lower the pH to 6.5. An acidic fertilizer solution (about 5.0 to 6.0 on the pH scale) is required to maintain the nutrient solution within a pH range of 5.5 to 6.5. Errors made in the nutrient solution mix or with pH level can be magnified. Be careful to monitor both the pH and nutrient level with a vigilant eye. Keep the nutrient solution "at the roots" between 5.5 and 6.5 for most plants to grow well.

According to Michael Dowgert, Ph. D. from Agro Dynamics, "Plants grown in rockwool do not suffer water stress until the rockwool is almost dry". But he also advises to never let rockwool dry out more than 50 percent. It is difficult to re-wet properly and roots will not grow in the dry spots.

Rockwool is somewhat forgiving. One hobby gardener reported that while away on vacation, the electricity went off at the home and the rockwool garden was not irrigated for eight days and nights. The plants growing in the slabs were very much alive upon her return, but the plants had not grown much. They also suffered from mild fertilizer (salt) burn. She changed the nutrient solution and watered a double cycle to flush out any fertilizer salt buildup and to ensure complete wetting of the slabs. The garden took off to grow a fine crop.

Rockwool stays so wet that algae grows on surfaces exposed to light. While this green algae is unsightly, it does not compete with plants for nutrition. If the algae turns black and slimy (decaying) it can harbor bacteria or viruses that can affect your plants. Harmless fungus gnats could also take up residence in this algae. Avoid the unsightly algae by covering the rockwool with plastic. Dead, decaying algae can also rob oxygen necessary for nutrient uptake. There are several algacides that can be added to the nutrient solution to control algae. Chemical algacides are not recommended for use with food crops. If you decide to use an algacide, read the label carefully to ensure it is not toxic to plants and use it *very sparingly*.

Rockwool manufacturers offer bats or slabs, propagation blocks or cubes, bulk or granular flock. Most cubes are wrapped in a plastic sleeve with open ends. The rockwool flock usually comes in three grades: coarse, medium and fine. The flock may also be either water repellent (like the insulation that it is designed after) or water absorbent.

The rockwool used for insulation is similar to the horticultural grade but it is the wrong density and quality for fast growing annuals. However it has been used as a soil amendment or to line hanging baskets, creating a water reservoir, with annual and perennial plants very successfully. Used as a soil additive, it retains moisture and facilitates drainage.

American brands are less expensive than imports, but to date imported rockwools offer a complete product line. American rockwool manufacturers are still working on more diverse products at competitive prices.

Grodan is one of the most popular brands of rockwool. Grodan is expensive because it is manufactured in Denmark and shipped across the ocean to the USA. Nichias Agriwool from Japan is becoming more popular in the U.S and is the brand of preference in British Columbia, Canada. Other brands include Capogro from Great Britain (also manufactured in the U.S.), Cultilene, French made rockwool, Basalan rockwool manufactured in Holland, Delta Grow rockwool made in Texas, Grow Gold rockwool from Alabama, Hortiwool from Indiana, Canadian rockwool, and Partek rockwool from Finland. Rockwool is also manufactured in Korea and Australia.

Most hydroponic retail suppliers have had some experience with rockwool and can usually give you hands on advice.

The Secret of Rockwool

Rockwool provides from 90 to 95 percent air space in between it's fibers. It holds more nutrient solution and more air than any other growing medium. High quality rockwool does not react to, or change the nutrient balance or mineral composition when nutrients are applied.

When rockwool is saturated, the ratio of water to air within the pores is

Rockwool is available in slabs, cubes and granular flock.

ideal for root growth; it contains about 80 percent nutrient solution, 15 percent air pore space and 5 percent rockwool fiber. These figures are approximate and may vary with different brands. With proper drainage, rockwool holds so much oxygen and drains so freely that it is virtually impossible to drown roots by overwatering.

The roots are bathed in a nutrient solution that offers perfect growing conditions. There is very little osmotic pressure (page 30) between the roots and the nutrient solution. The roots are able to draw in the maximum amount of nutrient solution.

A magnified cross section of rockwool.

CAUTION! Over-watering or drowning roots cuts off their oxygen. If the surface under the rockwool has low spots and the roots stand in stagnant "puddles" of water for over a few hours they may rot.

Leaching can be used regularly to control nutrition and salt buildup. A 10 to 30 percent overflow or flooding every week or two usually prevents fertilizer salt buildup.

Water concentrates in the lower half of the slab or cube. The capillary holding action of the rockwool will keep water in the slab or cube. Yet most of the water will concentrate in the lower one to two inches of the slab. There is little or no need to have a slab over three or four inches thick. The roots grow out the bottom and sides of the slab and rooting cubes. The roots will grow toward the bottom of the garden bed, between the plastic covering and the rockwool slab. The top part of the slab or cube serves as an anchor to the plants.

Commercial greenhouse growers apply 10 to 30 percent more nutrient solution than is taken up by the plant each watering so that any fertilizer (salt) buildup in the rockwool is washed away. They have few nutrient deficiencies, lush growth and high yields. Some hobby gardens are located where it is very difficult to let the solution run-off freely. Hobbyists with small gardens have found recirculating the nutrient solution works just fine. They top off the reservoir every few days with water or a mild mix of nutrient solution and change the solution weekly. The nutrient solution should be completely drained and changed every week or two if recirculation is used.

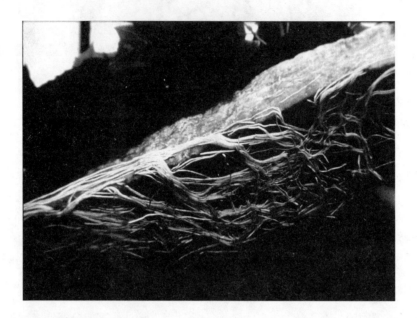

Strong healthy roots growing out the bottom of a slab.

Rockwool Is Safe

To ensure safety, there are some tricks to handling rockwool. Like peat moss, dry rockwool can be abrasive and act as a skin irritant. Take extra care if you have sensitive skin. Use gloves, goggles and a face mask or respirator when handling dry rockwool, especially in enclosed areas. Once the rockwool is thoroughly wet, it is safe and easy to work with; it creates no dust and does not irritate the skin. Misting the air when breaking up a large bail of dry flock will keep dust to a minimum. Keep dry rockwool out of the reach of children and pets. As a safety precaution, wash clothes thoroughly after prolonged use.
Rockwool fibers consist of single monofilament strands bunched together. These fibers will "not split lengthwise" to form thinner fibrils. The physical characteristics of rockwool are therefore different from dangerous materials such as asbestos. Asbestos fibers split lengthwise into ultra thin fibrils that penetrate the body and cell walls and the body has a very difficult time passing them or breaking them down. Rockwool fibers are much thicker and break across the length to yield a short fat fiber that the body can easily discharge.

Chapter Two

How a Plant Grows in Rockwool

The seed has an outside coating to protect the embryo plant and a supply of stored food is within. A healthy seed will germinate given moisture, heat and air. The seed's coating splits, a rootlet grows downward, and a sprout with seed leaves pushes upward in search of light.

The single root from the seed grows down and branches out, similar to the way the stem branches out above ground. Tiny rootlets draw in water and nutrients (elemental substances needed for life). Roots also anchor plants in the rockwool. As the plant matures, the roots take on specialized functions. The center and older mature portions contain a water transport system and may also store food. The tips of the roots produce elongating cells that continue to push farther and farther into the rockwool in a quest for more water and food. The single celled root hairs are the parts of the root that actually absorb water and nutrients. They must be in the presence of oxygen. Without water and air these frail root hairs will dry up and die. They are very delicate and may easily be damaged by light, air or careless hands if moved or exposed.

The stem also grows through elongation producing new buds along the stem. The central or terminal bud carries growth upward; side or lateral buds turn into branches or leaves. The stem transmits water and nutrients from the delicate root hairs to the growing buds leaves, and flowers. Sugars and starches, manufactured in the leaves, are distributed through the plant via the stem. This fluid flow takes place near the surface of the stem. If the stem is bound too tightly by string or other tie-downs, it will cut the flow of life-giving fluids. The stem also supports the plant with stiff cellulose, located in the inner walls.

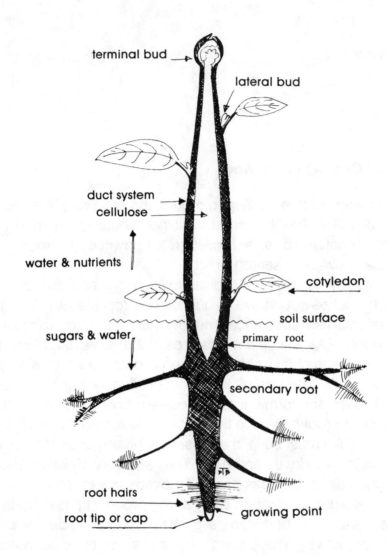

terminal bud

lateral bud

duct system

cellulose

water & nutrients

cotyledon

soil surface

sugars & water

primary root

secondary root

root hairs

root tip or cap

growing point

Once the leaves expand, they start to manufacture food (carbohydrates). Chlorophyll, the substance that gives plants their green color, converts carbon dioxide (CO_2) from the air, water, containing nutrients, and light energy into carbohydrates and oxygen. This process is called photosynthesis. It requires water drawn up from the roots, through the stem, into the leaves where it encounters CO_2. Tiny pores located on the underside of the leaf, called stomata or stoma funnel CO_2 into contact with the water. In order for photosynthesis to occur, the leaf's interior tissue must be kept moist. The stomata open and close to regulate the flow of moisture, preventing dehydration. Plant leaves are also protected from drying out by an outer skin. The stomata also permit the outflow of water vapor and oxygen taken in by the roots. The stomata and must be kept clean at all times to promote vigorous growth.

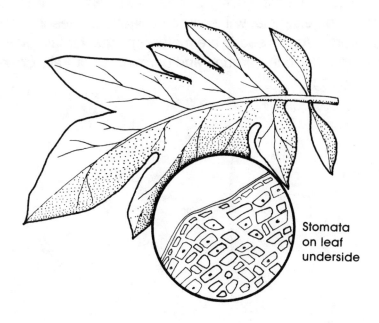

Stomata
on leaf
underside

Most flowers and vegetables will flower if conditions are right; for short-day plants, the main variable is the photoperiod.   Short day plants require twelve hours of darkness and twelve hours of light to bloom. Examples of short day plants are chrysanthemums, poinsettias and Christmas cacti. In the fall, the days become shorter and plants are signaled that the annual life cycle is coming to an end. The plant's functions change. Leafy growth slows and flowers start to form.

The majority of plants are long-day and bloom according to chronological age. That is, when they are two or three months old, they start to bloom. Flowers such as marigolds, petunias, pansies, cosmos, California poppies and zinnias will continue to bloom once flowering starts. Long-day vegetables will set blossoms that soon drop when fruit forms in the wake of the flower. Many common vegetables such as tomatoes, peppers, egg plants, squash etc. fall into this category. Leaf crops such as lettuce, spinach, basal, etc. are very productive indoors.

Monocious plants are either male or female. When both the female and male plants are in bloom, pollen from the male flower lands on the female flower, thereby fertilizing it. The male dies after producing and shedding as much pollen as possible. Hermaphrodite plants have both male and female flower parts on the same plant. The male easily pollinates the female part of the flower, but shaking tomatoes for example, will ensure pollination. Seeds form and grow within the female flowers. As the seeds are maturing, the female plant slowly dies. The mature seeds either fall to the ground and germinate naturally or are collected for planting the next spring.

Chapter Three

Water and Nutrients

Water and fertilizer work together to feed plants. Nutrients in fertilizer dissolve in water to form the nutrient solution. This water based solution carries nutrients through the plant. More than 75 percent of a plant's weight is water.

Tiny root hairs absorb water, nutrients and oxygen in the nutrient solution and carry them via the stem to the leaves. This flow of water from the soil through the plant is called transpiration. A fraction of the water is processed and used in photosynthesis, the remainder evaporates into the air, carrying waste products along with it, via the stomata in the leaves. Some of the water also returns manufactured sugars and starches to the roots.

Unfortunately, common tap water may contain high levels of alkaline salts, sulfur, chlorine or sodium and may have a pH out of the acceptable 5 to 6.5 range (page 41). Water containing sulfur is easily smelled and tasted. Saline water is more difficult to detect. Most water supplies contain some sodium and chlorine. Chlorine is used only in minute quantities by plants and rockwool will harbor buildup deposits unless there is regular flushing to leach out the excess salts. Sodium should not be used at all as it replaces potassium, a very necessary nutrient.

Water in coastal areas is generally full of salts that wash inland from the ocean. Many present day deserts are ancient lake beds where vast deposits of salts have built up and deposited. Water from these areas will also be full of undesirable salts. You can see these salts as they often buildup in and around shower heads and household water taps.

As you can see, the success of a rockwool garden depends on leaching or flushing out extra mineral salts should they accumulate.

Chlorine and sodium are added to many "soft" water systems. Small amounts of chlorine affect plant growth very little, but salt-softened water should be avoided. Too much salt will kill any plant. When sodium and chlorine buildup in the rockwool, they increase the conductivity (DS) (page 54) of the medium. At the higher DS, the plants take up sodium instead of vital potassium, calcium and magnesium. To find out if there is an excess of sodium or any other element, check your county or city water bureau analysis (page 21). If the sodium and chlorine register less than 50 parts per million (ppm) you probably have little to worry about. If the level is between at 50 and 70 ppm the stage is set for some nutrient problems. If the chloride (chlorine) or sodium content is above 100, do not use the water without filtration to remove the elements, which is very expensive. To remove chlorine from water, let it sit overnight in an open container. The chlorine will turn to a gas and evaporate when it comes in contact with the air. Heating or stirring the solution dissipates the chlorine faster.

Unlike soil and peat, unwanted salt buildup in rockwool is much less. However buildup can still occur. The main "nutrients" to buildup are sodium and chlorine and sometimes sulfates. An excess of these salts inhibits seed germination, burns root hairs and tips or edges of leaves, and stunts plant growth. Salt buildup in rockwool is easily controlled by flooding or leaching with weak nutrient solution regularly. Flushing will wash out toxic buildup of salts. It is a good idea to leach containers every week. Hard or well water may be very alkaline and usually contains notable amounts of calcium and magnesium. Both nutrients will be put to good use by flowering and fruiting plants. Hard (alkaline) water seldom contains enough calcium or magnesium to toxify rockwool. If the pH climbs above 7, the calcium can combine with the magnesium sulfate creating gypsum which is insoluble and renders the nutrients useless to the plants.

Rule of Thumb: 1) Leach small gardens weekly. 2) leach slabs daily 3) leach house plants monthly.

The water from your local water system is generally OK in most areas for small rockwool gardens, but if the water smells or tastes bad to you, plants probably will not like it either. If you have unsavory water or want a fine tuned garden, start with pure water. Add all the appropriate soluble nutrients to the solution.

This method is the simplest way to control the nutrient solution. Start with the purest water you can find. Measure out the exact amount of each mineral element and add to the water. This is easily done if you use a commercial "complete" plant nutrient specifically designed for growing in rockwool.

Another solution is to analyze the raw water (see water bureau printout page 21). After you have found the exact nutrient concentrations in the water, a nutrient solution can be mixed specifically for that water and whatever crop you are growing. There are many books that cover nutrient formulas very well. Please refer to your local library or bookstore for the books listed in the bibliography.

Most water, except rainwater, contains carbonate and bicarbonate, which will retain the pH higher than desired. The two ions and bicarbonate, in combination make up the "buffering capacity." A carbonate/bicarbonate solution of 30 to 50 parts per million (ppm) yields adequate buffering capacity, but not too much, to make the pH consistently too high. The buffering capacity keeps the pH on an even keel. An excess or high carbonate/bicarbonate causes the pH to remain consistently high.

Dolomite lime is applied to soil gardens to retain "sweet" soil and it adds calcium and magnesium in the process. Dolomite lime acts like carbonate/bicarbonate. It buffers the nutrients and keeps the soil's pH easy to manage.

Ask your local water bureau to send you a water analysis. The telephone number may be found under the special city or county section of the phone book if it is not listed alphabetically in the white pages.

Check the elements in the chart on the next pages against your local water analysis. If the nutrients in your water supply fall in any excess categories, consider using a fertilizer that has less of the already abundant nutrient, filter your water, or consider using a "custom formula".

The nutrients in the chart on the next pages should be included in the water analysis from the local water bureau. There are many other chemicals listed in the water analysis. These elements are not necessary for plant growth and can be ignored when they occur at low levels (below 5 parts per million).

For the most part, city water is OK to use as long as it does not have total dissolved solids (TDS) over 100 ppm.

Minimum and maximum mineral concentrations for fertilizer solution

	Minimum	Maximum
pH -	4.0	8.0
conductivity (DS)	< 100 ppm	
Nitrate-nitrogen	10	500
Phosphorus	40	100
Potassium Calcium	100	600
Calcium	100	100
Magnesium	50	150
Sodium	0	400
Chlorine	10	200
Sulphur	150	1000
Iron	0.5	5
Copper	0.5	1
Zinc	0.1	1
Manganese	0.5	10
Boron	0.1	1
Molybdenum	0.001	

Bicarbonate equivalent - equal to 500 - 1200 lbs./ton

Bicarbonate equivalent - equal to 500 - 1200 lbs./ton

If your water is over these levels, consider using a fertilizer that has less of this nutrient.

Water Filters

Filters or strainers remove debris from the irrigation system so that all water flows freely through pumps and drip emitters.

Inexpensive household water filters can be installed in the water line. They are rated for either cold or cold and hot water. Many people install one just below the kitchen sink. Filters are rated relative to the size micron of particle they can filter out. Household systems use a cotton filter to remove rust and dirt particles down to 25 microns. A cellulose fiber filter will remove down to five microns (two ten thousandths of an inch) and a charcoal filter will remove bad taste and smell. The best is a compressed block, activated charcoal. A granulated carbon filter is not recommended.

An in-line filter will remove debris
from the nutrient solution.

ANNUAL WATER ANALYSIS
January 1990
*Concentrations in Milligrams/Liter

	RAW WATER (1)	FINISHED WATER (2)	EPA REGULATIONS (3) PRIMARY	SECONDARY
Alkalinity (as $CaCO_3$)	7.5	6.50		
Hydroxide (as $CaCO_3$)	0	0		
Carbonate (as $CaCO_3$)	0	0		
Bicarbonate (as $CaCO_3$)	7.5	6.5		
Color (standard units)	<5	<5		15
Hardness (as $CaCO_3$)	7.0	7.7		
pH	7.02	6.83		6.5-8.5
Total Solids (@ 180°C)	22.1	19.3		500
Filtrable Solids	21.7	18.70		
Non-Filtrable Solids	0.40	0.60		
Fixed Solids (@ 550°C)	15.5	12.3		
Specific Conductance (micromhos per cm @ 25°C)	21.5	24.2		
Turbidity (NTU)	0.22	0.44	1.0	
Aluminum (Al)	0.051	0.058		
Ammonia Nitrogen (NH_3-N)	<0.020	0.063		
Arsenic (As)	<0.001	<0.001	0.05	
Barium (Ba)	<0.001	<0.001	1.0	
Cadmium (Cd)	<0.001	<0.001	0.010	
Calcium (Ca)	1.66	1.91		
Carbon Dioxide, Free (CO_2)	2.0	2.8		
Carbon Dioxide, Total (CO_2)	8.6	8.5		
Chloride (Cl)	0.5	1.0		250.0
Chromium (Cr)	<0.001	<0.001	0.05	
Copper (Cu)	0.003	0.120		1.0
Cyanide (CN)	<0.005	<0.005		
Fluoride (F)	<0.04	<0.04		
Iron (Fe)	0.062	0.060		0.3
Lead (Pb)	<0.001	<0.001	0.05	
Magnesium (Mg)	0.69	0.72		
Manganese (Mn)	0.008	0.010		0.05
Mercury (Hg)	<0.001	<0.001	0.002	
Nitrate Nitrogen (NO_3-N)	0.049	0.066	10	
Nitrite Nitrogen (NO_2-N)	<0.001	<0.001		
Nitrogen, Kjeldahl (N)	0.069	0.043		
Phosphate - Reactive (PO_4-P)	<0.003	<0.003		
Phosphorus, Total (P)	0.004	0.005		
Potassium (K)	0.22	0.25		
Selenium (Se)	<0.001	<0.001	0.01	
Silica (Si)	4.24	4.43		
Silver (Ag)	<0.001	<0.001	0.05	
Sodium (Na)	1.34	1.42		
Sulfate (SO_4)	0.3	0.3		250
Zinc (Zn)	0.001	0.001		5
Tannin - & Lignin-like compounds as tannic acid	0.24	0.16		
Methylene Blue Active Substances (MBAS)	<0.025	<0.025		
Total Organic Carbon (TOC)	1.54	1.73		
Total Trihalomethanes (annual running average)		0.0080	0.100	

* All concentrations in milligrams/liter unless otherwise noted

Methods from EPA-600/4-79-020 "Methods for Chemical Analysis of Water and Wastes."

(1)   Raw Water sampled at Headworks, Bull Run Reserve by Water Bureau Personnel.

(2)   Finished water sampled at Portland Building, 1120 SW 5th Avenue, Portland, Oregon by Water Bureau Personnel.

(3)   Oregon Administrative Rules, Chapter 333, Public Water Systems, 1983.

KC:dmh   WP:89-WQANAL (WQZ-01)

An in-line filter or strainer will keep unwanted debris out of your garden. Install a good strainer (80 mesh or smaller line filter and clean regularly) to remove debris that could collect and clog or plug drip emitters. One of the biggest obstacles in a drip system is dirt that sticks in the emitters. Clogged emitters flow at different rates. This variation irrigates plants unevenly. There are two ways to counter this situation, after a stainless steel or plastic screen is installed. 1. Use a high pressure pump and maintain enough pressure in the system to flush any debris or salt buildup out of the nozzle. 2. Use a low pressure pump with no restrictions at the emitter.

A household plastic scouring pad or folded nylon stocking works well to filter drain or pump intakes. Just secure in place with a rubber band.

Nutrients

Over twenty elements are needed for a plant to grow. Carbon, hydrogen and oxygen are absorbed from the air and water. The rest of the elements, called mineral nutrients, are dissolved in the nutrient solution. The primary or macro-nutrients (nitrogen (N), phosphorus (P) and potassium (K)) are the elements plants use the most.

Calcium (Ca) and magnesium (Mg) are secondary nutrients and used in smaller amounts. Iron (Fe), sulfur (S), manganese (Mn), boron (B), molybdenum (Mo), zinc (Zn) and copper (Cu) are micro-nutrients or trace elements. Trace elements are found in most soils. Rockwool fertilizers must contain these trace elements, as they do not normally exist in sufficient quantities in rockwool or water.

Other elements also play a part in plant growth. Aluminum, chlorine, cobalt, iodine, selenium, silicon, sodium and vanadium are not normally included in nutrient mixes. They are required in very minute amounts that are usually present as impurities in the water supply or mixed along with other nutrients.

NOTE: The nutrients must be soluble (able to be dissolved in water) and go into solution.

Macro-nutrients

Nitrogen (N) is primary to plant growth. Plants convert nitrogen to make proteins essential to new cell growth. Nitrogen is mainly responsible for leaf and stem growth as well as overall size and vigor. Nitrogen moves easily to active young buds, shoots and leaves and slower to older leaves.

Deficiency signs show first in older leaves. They turn a pale yellow and may die. New growth becomes weak and spindly. An abundance of nitrogen will cause soft, weak growth and even delay flower and fruit production if it is allowed to accumulate.

Phosphorus (P) is necessary for photosynthesis and works as a catalyst for energy transfer within the plant. Phosphorus helps build strong roots and is vital for flower and seed production. Highest levels of phosphorus are used during germination, seedling growth and flowering.

Deficiencies will show in older leaves first. Leaves turn deep green on a uniformly smaller, stunted plant. Leaves show brown or purple spots.

NOTE: Phosphorus flocculates when concentrated and combined with calcium.

Potassium (K) activates the manufacture and movement of sugars and starches, as well as growth by cell division. Potassium increases chlorophyll in foliage and helps regulate stomata openings so plants make better use of light and air. Potassium encourages strong root growth, water uptake and triggers enzymes that fight disease. Potassium is necessary during all stages of growth. It is especially important in the development of fruit.

Deficiency signs of potassium are: plants are the tallest and appear healthy. Older leaves mottle and yellow between veins, followed by whole leaves that turn dark yellow and die. Flower and fruit drop are common problems associated with potassium deficiency. Potassium is usually locked out by high salinity.

Secondary Nutrients

Magnesium (Mg) is found as a central atom in the chlorophyll molecule and is essential to the absorption of light energy. Magnesium aids in the utilization of nutrients, neutralizes acids and toxic compounds produced by the plant.

Deficiency signs of magnesium are: Older leaves yellow from the center outward, while veins remain green on deficient plants. Leaf tips may discolor and curl upward. Growing tips turn lime green if the deficiency progresses to the top of the plant.

Calcium (Ca) is fundamental to cell manufacture and growth. Soil gardeners use dolomite lime, which contains calcium and magnesium, to keep the soil sweet or buffered. Rockwool gardeners use calcium to buffer excess nutrients. Calcium moves slowly within the plant and tends to concentrate in roots and older growth. Consequently young growth shows deficiency signs first.

Deficient leaf tips, edges and new growth will turn brown and die back. If too much calcium is applied early in life, it will stunt growth as well. It will also flocculate when a concentrated form is combined with potassium.

Trace Elements

Sulphur (S) is a component of plant proteins and plays a role in root growth and chlorophyll supply. Distributed relatively evenly with largest amounts in leaves which affects the flavor and odor in many plants.

Sulphur, like calcium, moves little within plant tissue and the first signs of a deficiency are pale young leaves. Growth is slow but leaves tend to get brittle and stay narrower than normal.

Iron (Fe) is a key catalyst in chlorophyll production and is used in photosynthesis. A lack of iron turns leaves pale yellow or white while the veins remain green. Iron is difficult for plants to absorb and moves slowly within the plant. Always use chelated (immediately available to the plant) iron in nutrient mixes.

Manganese (Mg) works with plant enzymes to reduce nitrates before producing proteins. A lack of manganese turns young leaves a mottled yellow or brown.

Zinc (Z) is a catalyst and must be present in minute amounts for plant growth. A lack of zinc results in stunting, yellowing and curling of small leaves. An excess of zinc is uncommon but very toxic and causes wilting or death.

Copper (C) is a catalyst for several enzymes. A shortage of copper makes new growth wilt and causes irregular growth. Excesses of copper causes sudden death. Copper is also used as a fungicide and wards off insects and diseases because of this property.

Boron (B) is necessary for cells to divide and protein formation. It also plays an active role in pollination and seed production.

Molybdenum (Mn) helps form proteins and aids the plant's ability to fix nitrogen from the air. A deficiency causes leaves to turn pale and fringes to appear scorched. Irregular leaf growth may also result.

These nutrients are mixed together to form a complete plant fertilizer. The mix contains all the nutrients in the proper ratios to give plants all they need for lush, rapid growth. The fertilizer is dissolved in water to make a nutrient solution. Water transports these soluble nutrients into contact with the plant roots. In the presence of oxygen and water, the nutrients are absorbed through the root hairs.

Nutrient Disorders

Nutrient disorders are caused by too much or too little of one or several nutrients being available. These nutrients are made available between a pH range of 5 and 7 and a dissolved solids (DS) range of 800 to 3,000 ppm. Maintaining these conditions is the key to proper nutrient uptake.

Regular maintenance of the proper nutrient solution and pH helps to prevent serious nutrient deficiencies or excesses. The list of nutrients (page 19) gives both toxicity and deficiency symptoms for each nutrient. Rockwool acts like a large sponge that absorbs nutrients. They stay there like soap in a sponge until the roots absorb them. Flushing these nutrients out regularly, like soap is flushed or wrung from a sponge, will prevent nutrient imbalances. Flushing and changing the nutrient solution regularly is the best way to keep a garden growing strong healthy plants and avoid problems. Changing the nutrient solution often maintains the proper "hydroponic balance".

A pH fluctuation could create a nutrient deficiency. Likewise a nutrient imbalance could create a pH change. It may be difficult to determine the exact cause of a disorder. What if two or more elements are deficient at the same time or there is a toxic level of some unknown element? When difficult-to-diagnose problems occur, change the nutrient solution. This will correct the problem and supply the missing elements. If the problem persists, change fertilizer mixes. The plants do not have to be diagnosed, just treated. Plants sometimes respond to nutrient changes slowly and it could take up to a week for the garden to respond to a fresh or new nutrient mix.

A sample of the nutrient solution and plant tissue can be analyzed by a laboratory, which is expensive and time consuming. Then the exact nutrient mix would have to be formulated to correct the problem. It's much easier to change the nutrient solution.

Check water quality (page 21) - look for sodium and chlorine. Also look for dry pockets in the rockwool root zone. Check for even wetting and drainage. Look for fungus and insect damage on the roots and leaves respectively. The roots should be white or light tan with fine root hairs. Brown, black or "jelly-like" roots are a sign of root disease.

 Rule of Thumb: If the garden has a nutrient disorder, change the nutrient solution and adjust the pH.

Nutrient disorders will occur to all the plants at the same time if they are receiving the same solution. Climatic disorders - windburn, lack of light, temperature stress, fungus and insect damage - usually show up on individual plants that are most affected. For example, plants that are next to a heat vent may show signs of heat scorch. Or a hanging basket in an exposed location may show signs of sun burn.

Fertilizers

The nutrients in fertilizers are described by one or two letters. In the case of primary nutrients, N-P-K are always listed in the same order and express the percentage of each nutrient contained in the fertilizer. The N-P-K are listed by numbers on front of the fertilizer label. For example a fertilizer that shows 23-19-17 has 23 percent (N) nitrogen, 19 percent (P) phosphorus and 17 percent (K) potassium. The secondary and trace elements are usually listed in the "Guaranteed Analysis" on the label of the fertilizer.

The objective of fertilization is to provide a constant supply of all necessary nutrients in optimum ratios.

Rockwool fertilizers require a complete and balanced formula. A complete fertilizer contains all of the macro- and micro-nutrients.

NOTE: No nutrients can be available over the maximum limits or toxicity symptoms, reverse osmosis, salt buildup and nutrient lockup become problems. See Chart on page 19.

Any complete fertilizer will work with rockwool. Several specialty rockwool fertilizers are made by smaller manufacturers and some growers mix their own. If you use over 250 pounds of fertilizer per year, it is worth mixing your own. Premixed fertilizers purchased from the garden center are formulated by professionals and are much easier to use.

Rule of Thumb: Buy a premixed fertilizer if you use less than 250 pounds per year.

Slow growing house plants are not as fussy as fast growing annual flowers and vegetables. A simple all purpose house plant fertilizer mix can be made by combining soluble trace elements with a soluble general purpose fertilizer which forms a complete fertilizer. Be sure the "guaranteed analysis" on the fertilizer label contains at least 10 or 11 of these natural elements.

Chelated nutrients are available immediately to the plant. Chelated fertilizers speed nutrient uptake by roots.

Peters Hydrosol, EcoGrow, Hydrolife, DynaGro, and General Hydroponics are examples of just a few commercial hydroponic fertilizers. Any complete mix is OK. For more information see the Bibliography. Many of these fertilizers are two part formulas and each brand has different mixing instructions.

Whatever fertilizer you decide to use, keep it dry! It will combine (flocculate) and separate into worthless slop if allowed to get wet. Store in a cool dry place. Always read the directions completely before using.

For the best rockwool nutrient solution, you should use rainwater, distilled water or purified water that does not contain added salts.

Many rockwool fertilizers are a two part formula. One part contains the phosphate source and the other part contains the calcium source. Calcium, and phosphorus must be kept separate when concentrated. They do not cause any problems when in dilute solution, but in a concentrated form, the two will flocculate, or combine into a worthless mud that settles on the bottom of the reservoir.

There are many good hydroponic fertilizers to choose from.

Rule of Thumb: Use a two part solution for high performance gardens.

Organic Fertilizers

Organic nutrients contain a carbon molecule and non-organic or chemical nutrients have no carbon molecule. This simple difference distinguishes organic and chemical fertilizers. Once the organic fertilizer is taken up by the roots, the organic nutrients are changed to mineral elements and compounds.

More soluble organic fertilizers.

Organic fertilizers can be used to fertilize rockwool gardens but are not as common. Some organic nutrients are more difficult to dissolve and the amount of available minerals can not be controlled or analyzed easily. Bat and seabird guanos, livestock manures, fish emulsion and liquid seaweed are examples of some water soluble fertilizers used in an organic fertilizer mix. The organic fertilizers are mixed with water and strained through a cheese cloth or a nylon stocking before being applied to the rockwool. The straining ensures the organic tea or nutrient solution will not contain large chunks of insoluble elements that plug narrow tubing or emitters. Plants extract and process mineral elements from organic materials, unused elements must be flushed out. Guanos, fish emulsion and poultry manures are potentially dangerously high in nitrogen (NH_4) and should be added sparingly.

The Nutrient Solution

The idea behind a rockwool nutrient solution is simple: apply a mild nutrient solution that constantly supplies nutrients in an available form. The plant uses the nutrients it needs, the rest is flushed away by new nutrient with each irrigation

Bat guano is one of the best high phosphorus water soluble organic fertilizers available.

cycle. Excess nutrients are flushed away and never get a chance to concentrate or buildup. In small gardens, recycle the nutrient solution and change weekly. Larger or high performance gardens run a nutrient solution through only once and flush by over-watering 10 to 30 percent with each feeding.

A hydroponic nutrient solution, fertilizer dissolved in water, supplies all the food a plant needs. The rate that the nutrient solution is taken up by the plant dictates the growth rate providing all other needs are fulfilled. Nutrient uptake is fastest when adequate oxygen is available to the roots while in the presence of the nutrient solution. After the nutrient solution is applied to the rockwool, it drains away providing air pockets, so the oxygen can work with the roots to draw in the nutrients.

To aerate the nutrient solution (give it more oxygen) simply pour it through the air. Every time water moves through the air, it picks up oxygen. An aquarium air stone or bubbler can also be placed in the reservoir for added aeration.

Nutrients are taken-up at different rates by the plant. This uneven nutrient uptake gives some nutrients in the solution a chance to buildup to toxic levels. Nutrient solution that is recirculated over a week or two, coupled with evaporation and transpiration, make it almost impossible to "top off" a nutrient reservoir with water or to guess how much of a specific nutrient is used. To accurately replenish a nutrient solution in a recirculating system, each nutrient must be measured and added. A dissolved solids (DS) meter (page 47) can be useful to determine if you have a toxic salt buildup.

 Rule of Thumb: Let nutrient solution drain to waste or change and flush once every week or two. Catch the "waste" fertilizer for use on your house plants or outdoor garden.

Rockwool gardens can be very high-performance, creating phenomenal plant growth. If something malfunctions, say the electricity goes off, the pump breaks, the drain gets clogged with roots, or there is a rapid fluctuation in the pH, the growth could slow to a halt. A repeated mistake could kill or stunt plants so badly that they never fully recover. High performance rockwool gardens provide the means of supplying the proper amount of nutrients plants need. If misused, plants can starve to death or be over-feed in a short period of time.

Osmosis

The nutrient solution is drawn in through the entire plant by a process called osmosis. Osmosis is the tendency of fluids to pass through a semi-permeable membrane and mix with each other. The semi-permeable membranes in the root hairs will allow fluids carrying nutrients to pass through but filter out impurities.

The root hairs contain a saline solution full of organic acids. This solution attracts the stronger nutrient solution outside the semi-permeable membrane.

Osmosis can also reverse! In this situation the nutrient solution is weaker (less concentrated) than the solution inside the plant. This condition causes the water to be drawn out from the roots resulting in severe wilt, until the plant actually dehydrates to the point of death! The most dynamic example of reverse osmosis is found with cut Christmas trees. The trunk of the cut tree may not be able to produce an adequate solution to attract the water in the bottom of the tray. If the water in the tray is less saline, it will actually pull the water from the tree! The more water given the tree, the more the solution pulls the water from the tree. When the concentration of mineral salts in a nutrient solution is too weak, the chance of reverse osmosis increases.

Roots hairs are very healthy in rockwool. They have much surface area for the osmotic exchange to take place. The solution in the numerous root hairs draw in even more nutrient solution. Healthy strong roots make for a healthy, strong plant.

Temperature

The ideal temperature range of the nutrient solution is between 65 and 70 deg. F (21 deg. C). Heating the nutrient solution during cool months will help boost plant performance. For every 10 deg. F (5 deg. C) the heat raises, the rate of photosynthesis increases double until 85 to 95 deg. F (30 to 35 deg. C) has been reached. Never let the nutrient solution temperature get higher than 85 degrees F (30 deg. C) or below 95 degrees F (35 deg. C). If roots get too hot or cold, they do not perform properly and may be damaged.

An aquarium heater or soil heating cables are often used to heat the nutrient solution. Run a ground wire into the nutrient solution if the aquarium heater or heating cables are not grounded. Attach the other end of the ground wire to a cold water pipe or metal stake driven into the earth to complete the ground. Always use a submersible heater large enough to heat the entire volume of water in the reservoir without burning out (see chart below). It may take several hours for the heating cables or heater to raise the temperature in a large volume of solution.

Suggested watts per gallon a heater should be to heat nutrient solution

    10 - 30 gallons = 100 watt heater
    30 - 60 gallons = 150 watt heater
    60 - 120 gallons = 250 watt heater

The chart above lists the suggested size of heater to use under normal conditions.

Submersible aquarium heaters have an adjustable thermostat. They are safe for fish and give off no harmful residues that are harmful to plants. Many insulated soil heating cables are equipped with a built in thermostat that is generally pre-set to about 72 degrees F (22 deg. C). Some gardeners use these cables to heat the nutrient solution. They place the heating cables in the reservoir. The cables, even though coiled, do not overheat because the nutrient solution disperses the heat evenly. However, few soil heating cables are grounded. The larger gardens can use a a household water heater element attached to a thermostat.

Heaters   may burn out if the reservoir goes dry for more than a few minutes. The element, not surrounded by water, tries to heat the entire volume of air in the room. A non-submersible heater may burn out if submerged. Do not touch the heater element when it is out of the water: it heats up and may burn you severely.

In hydroponic gardens where the nutrient solution is pumped completely out of the reservoir, place the aquarium heater into a gallon jar full of water or it will overheat and break when the cool nutrient solution flows back into the tank.

Never place heating cables directly against the rockwool. Always have a pad, sand, or something to transfer heat between the rockwool and the electric cable. The heat from the cable will fry the roots and dry out small portions of the rockwool.

Water retains heat or cold for a long time. Water barrels painted black will absorb heat from the sun and are used as solar heat banks or collectors in greenhouses. They are lined up in a sunny location under the benches to heat up during the day and cool slowly at night. The water cools slower than the air and gives off heat.   The reverse is also true. Once cold, water stays cold. Setting the reservoir up on a piece of Styrofoam will help insulate the bottom against cold concrete floors.

The nutrient solution should be replaced with water that is at least 60 deg. F (15 deg. C).   Cold water will shock delicate roots. Cold 40-degree F 5-deg. C) water may take a day or two to warm up.

Reservoirs

The larger the reservoir the better.   It should hold 25 to 50 percent more nutrient solution than it takes to fill the garden beds or irrigate slabs to compensate for evaporation and transpiration.   The larger the volume of nutrient solution,   the more forgiving and the easier it is to control. Plants use much more water than nutrients; more water evaporates from uncovered rockwool gardens than covered gardens. Anticipate a water loss of 5 to 25 percent daily, depending on climate conditions and the size of plants. For example, a fast growing vegetable garden with a 30-gallon reservoir uses from 3-9 gallons a day. Three hot days in a row may cause a reservoir to run dry. Rockwool can be covered with plastic and a top placed on the reservoir to reduce evaporation.

The reservoir can be any size or shape as long as it holds water and doesn't react to chemicals. Plastic storage bins, Rubbermaid trays, large wooden bins lined with 20 mil plastic (water bed liner), even an old bath tub, make excellent reservoirs. A large galvanized livestock water trough will hold hundreds of gallons of solution. Galvanized trough should not be used unless lined with heavy (10 to 20 mil) plastic. Large greenhouses use a concrete pit under the greenhouse for a reservoir. The pit is coated with an inert paint. A plastic trash can is easy to drill and install a on/off valve at the bottom. Children's swimming pools hold a large volume of nutrient solution and are economical. They can keep the environment very humid but should be covered with a large piece of plastic to prevent evaporation and algae growth.

The concentration of elements in the solution increases when the water is

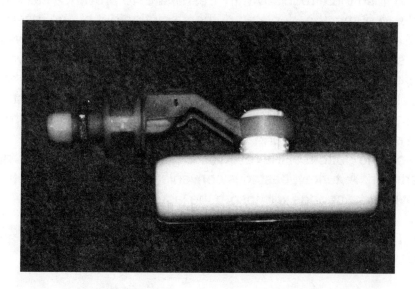

One of the many different float valves used to automatically fill the reservoir.

used; there is less water in the solution and nearly the same amount of nutrients, which concentrates the amount of fertilizer to unacceptable levels. More sophisticated gardens have a float valve (see photo) that adds more water as it is used from the reservoir. In manual systems, a "full" line on the inside of the reservoir tank shows when the solution is low. Water is manually added daily or as soon as the solution level drops.

If water is not replaced, the level of iron can increase up to three fold and the level of magnesium can easily double. A recirculating garden uses more calcium and potassium than non-recovery gardens. Other nutrient levels usually remain relatively constant. The pH and DS readings measure overall change in the nutrient solution. Do not assume that the pH or DS will remain constant. Remember that the garden is using some of the nutrients each time they cycle through. This concentrates and changes the nutrients, thereby changing the pH. It almost always raises the pH. The pH should be checked and adjusted accordingly.

Small reservoirs are easy to pick up and empty into the sink, toilet or back yard. The depleted nutrient solution must be drained or pumped from larger reservoirs. If you have a vegetable garden, flower bed or lawn, use the spent nutrient on them as the solution still contains many of beneficial nutrients.

Attach a hose to the pump and pump the depleted nutrient solution out of the reservoir. Do not drain depleted nutrients into a septic tank. Nitrates and other nutrients disrupt the chemistry of the septic tank causing it to back up and overflow. Do not use this depleted nutrient solution repeatedly on containerized plants unless you flush them regularly with fresh water to prevent a salt buildup.

If unable to pump the depleted nutrient solution out of the reservoir, siphon it out. Careful! A mouthful of solution is unpleasant. An easy way to start the siphon is to submerge the entire hose so that it fills with water. Put your thumb over one end of the hose to form an air lock. Remove the covered end of the hose and place it below the level of the reservoir. The hose full of nutrient solution will begin to siphon when you remove your thumb. Remember, a siphon only works when the outlet is below the input end.

Sludge on the bottom of the reservoir is generally inert and will not react with the new fertilizer. A turkey baster is convenient to pick up the solution that the pump won't move and a sponge will absorb the last little bit of solution.

 Rule of Thumb: Check the level of the reservoir regularly and replenish with water as needed.

The depleted nutrient solution can be used to fertilize the outdoor garden. Do not dump the runoff in the same location repeatedly. It will buildup in the soil causing a toxic salt burn. In extreme cases the runoff may pollute ground water. Please be careful.

Pumps

Inexpensive submersible pumps are ideal for hydroponic rockwool gardens. You may find submersible pumps at many hardware stores and garden centers.

Pumps are rated by the gallons per hour (GPH) they can move, the pounds per square inch (PSI) under which they can operate and the maximum of height or "head" they can lift the solution. If you know the maximum head a pump delivers, just divide that figure by 2.31 to get the PSI of the pump. For example, a pump with a 6-foot head divided by 2.31 yields a PSI rating of 2.6. A pump with a head of 40 feet divided by 2.31 yields a rating of 17.32 PSI. City water pressure is usually delivered at 50 to 80 PSI.

Generally, the higher the water is lifted, the lower the volume. For example, a 275 GPH pump will lift 275 GPH one foot high in one hour, 225 GPH at a three-foot head, 200 GPH at a five-foot head and 25 GPH nine feet high.

A 1250 GPH pump that attaches to a garden hose (left) and a smaller 150 GPH pump.

The amount of electricity most small pumps use is negligible and they do not run very long.

Using a pump that supplies 20 to 50 percent more capacity than necessary keeps it from being over worked. For example, to fill a 20-gallon garden bed in less than 10 minutes and lift it 3 feet from the bottom of a reservoir, use a submersible pump that delivers at least 150 GPH.

To find the proper pump for your hydroponic garden use the following formula.

Gallons in garden bed / time to fill garden bed = GPM X 60 minutes = ??? GPH pump

To supply 20 gallons in 10 minutes and lift it 3 feet:

20 gallons/10 minutes = 2 gallons per minute

2 gallons per minute x 60 minutes = 120 GPH

Use a pump that delivers 120 GPH or more.

CHART Various pumps delivering water over one foot high to various drip emitters.

GPH head at different heights

1'	3'	5'	7'	9'
120	70	40	-	-
170	130	70	-	-
205	170	120	40	-
300	250	200	160	110
500	350	280	200	150
700	520	350	280	200

The chart is approximate, different brands of pumps will vary. The size of tubing will also affect the GPH: the larger the tubing, the more GPH, the smaller the tubing, the less GPH.

Pump GPH	1.0 GPH Emitter	0.5 GPH Emitter	0.3 GPH Emitter
40	20	35	40
70	35	70	120
120	50	100	150
150	70	150	200
170	80	170	300
200	90	200	300
250	120	300	400
350	150	400	600
500	200	600	800

Small pumps loose efficiency very quickly while high volume pumps continue to lift almost as much solution at various heights.

Small, inexpensive, low volume pumps loose pressure and volume rapidly and are suited for fewer drip emitters. Having less pressure, the friction of the hose is much greater, giving less nutrient flow.

More expensive pumps are available that handle corrosive, hot and cold materials. A pH lower than 5 could corrode metal parts on inexpensive pumps. These "non-corrosive pumps" should be considered if your pH runs at or below 5.

Stainless steel is the safest metal to use in a hydroponic rockwool system. It will not corrode when it comes into contact with the acidic nutrient solution. Most metals corrode and give off chemical elements as a by-product. These undesirable chemicals are taken up by the plant and could kill them.

Numerous small pumps that use small galvanized screws. These screws do not corrode enough to alter the nutrient solution and do not present a problem. A pH lower than 5 however will corrode most metals rapidly. Copper and brass pipes, fittings and parts should be avoided.

Many submersible pump housings are cast aluminum covered with an impermeable epoxy paint. The motor may be sealed in a non (electrical) conducting oil. Be careful if you decide to open an oil bathed pump for internal inspection. The oil may leak out when the motor casing is removed.

Make sure the garden is designed to keep the pump submerged to prevent air lock. Also, watch out for unwanted siphoning when reservoir is located above the emitters. After the pump is turned off, the nutrient solution will continue to siphon through the pump and down the supply line if just one emitter is below the reservoir. An anti-siphon valve can be used to stop this siphoning action or the reservoir can be moved below the level of the emitter.

Other submersible pumps are not bathed in oil. These types of submersible pumps and may overheat and burn up if operated while not submerged. Check the pump's instructions to find a pump that shuts off when out of water or use a shut-off type float valve.

A pump basket or a plastic kitchen scouring pad set around the pump will filter out large debris.

High pressure, high volume pumps are used for larger gardens. Most of these pumps are not submersible, have a higher horsepower rating and their GPH capacity stays relatively constant the higher the water is lifted. Some are self priming and others are not. Cost ranges from $200 to $800 for larger pumps that will not corrode and affect the nutrient solution. If buying a larger pump, consult the supplier and study the specifications carefully.

For example, a high volume pump with a stronger motor, delivering 200 GPH could service 180 one-GPH emitters or 360-.5 GPH drip emitters and still retain adequate pressure.

Garden Beds

For large ebb and flow gardens (page 61), it's necessary to calculate how much nutrient solution the garden bed will hold and use a reservoir that will hold 25 to 50 percent more. The extra volume is the necessary to compensate for evaporation and transpiration and to provide some leaching action. Measure the volume of liquid that the garden bed holds when it is full of rockwool.

To calculate the amount of nutrient solution the garden bed can hold when it is totally flooded, multiply the length X width X depth. For example a table that is 48 X 24 X 6 inches has a volume of 6912 cubic inches. One cubic foot is 12 X 12 X 12 inches = 1728 cubic inches. So 6912/1728 inches = 4 cubic feet. There are 7.48 gallons in a cubic foot. So 4 feet X 7.48 gallons = 30 gallons + 25 percent of 30 = 7.5 = 30 + 7.5 = 37.5 gallons of nutrient is needed.

A more simple, fool-proof way to calculate the necessary reservoir capacity is to fill the garden bed with pre-wet rockwool, flood the table to the desired depth, then measure the runoff.

The easiest way to ensure the garden bed does not overflow is to install an overflow port. The nutrient solution floods the garden bed up to the port and the port drains the excess nutrient solution back into the reservoir. The irrigation cycle fills the bed with one to two inches of nutrient solution. The port should be large enough (one to two inches) that a large volume of water drains easily.

The garden bed or ebb and flow table should fill within 5 to 15 minutes and drain slightly slower (10 to 20 minutes).
NOTE: If it drains out as fast as it is pumped in, the bed will never fill.

Flood the table one to twenty times daily depending on how fast roots dry out, temperature, size, number of plants and the desired growth rate all affect the irrigation frequency. Natural wind or a fan blowing on the garden speeds nutrient solution evaporation and transpiration. This causes the nutrient to be taken up by the roots more rapidly.

An adequate drain is difficult to find. Some of the best drains are stainless steel sink drains found at hardware stores.

To prevent roots and debris from clogging the drain, place a nylon stocking or a small mesh (quarter-inch or less) screen made from a non-corrosive material, over the drain. The screen should be easy to remove and clean. A plastic kitchen scouring pad makes a great drain and overflow port filter.

The Irrigation Cycle

Rockwool has a broad range of water holding capacities. It acts like a water bank for the roots. Water is deposited or saved until needed, then withdrawn by the roots. Rockwool may hold enough water and nutrients for several weeks. House plants for example, can be watered every 2 to 4 weeks. Irrigation frequency depends on the type and size of plants, temperature, light, etc. and how fast you want your garden to grow. But remember, do not let the plants wilt.

Plants that require a well drained medium can benefit from a mix of 50/50 water repellent and water absorbant rockwool flock.

Some high performance gardens are irrigated as often as once an hour, while others are irrigated a few minutes one to four times per day with excellent results.

During and soon after irrigation, the nutrient content of the bed and reservoir are about the same concentration. As the time passes between irrigations, the nutrient concentration and the pH gradually change. If enough time passes between waterings, the nutrient concentration may change so much that the plant is not able to absorb nutrients properly.

 Rule of Thumb: To check a cube for maximum moisture content, pick it up so that one corner is lower than the other 3. A few drops of nutrient solution will trickle from a block that is totally saturated.

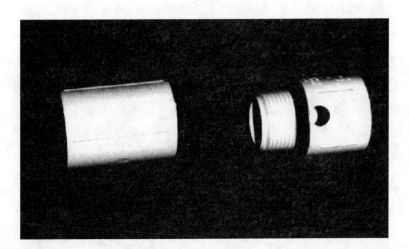

This combination drain/overflow port drains water out the small hole. When the growing bed is full, the excess nutrient solution spills over the top.

Roots in some ebb and flow gardens are so exposed to the air they should be irrigated every hour. For more on ebb and flow irrigation, see page 57. The section below on drip irrigation also contains many basic principles common to ebb and flow irrigation.

Drip Irrigation

Drip irrigation revolutionized desert farming. It moved from Israel in the 60's to California and Arizona in the 70's and into the greenhouse industry by the 80's. Now drip irrigation is becoming a popular way to irrigate house plants and hobby gardens all across America.

Gravity flow or a pump delivers the pre-mixed nutrient solution through a larger supply hose connected to a spaghetti tubing or drip emitter. Several factors dictate whether to use a large high volume pump, an inexpensive low volume pump or let gravity supply the water pressure.

The high pressure drip emitters must be operated at greater pressure than a small pump can generate. Low pressure drip emitters employ spaghetti tubing with little restriction at the emitter to deliver solution.

The fast flowing labyrinth type nozzle is a favorite for larger gardens of 100 emitters or more on a high volume pump. The labyrinth emitters deliver the same amount of solution to each plant and do not clog easily. The pressure in the system flushes debris through the nozzles.

For more information about larger drip systems, please refer to "Hydroponic Food Production" by Howard H. Resh, Woodbridge Press or "Rockwool in Horticulture" by Dennis L. Smith, Grower Books.

Water in small amounts, and often, to achieve fastest growth. Plants grow best with a consistent water supply. If more water uptake is necessary, increase the number of waterings. Each irrigation cycle delivers the same volume. There are more waterings during the heat of the day. Europeans apply a small amount of nutrient solution 10 to 20 times a day for maximum growth. Enough excess solution is applied to obtain a 10 to 30 percent leaching effect every day.

On a hot summer day, during prime growing conditions, each mature plant may take up several quarts of water per day. Irrigating the garden 10 to

20 times a day may be necessary for maximum water and nutrient uptake.

Some drip systems are able to deliver a pint or less per feeding. The key to irrigating 10 to 20 times every 24 hours is having a drip system that delivers solution to all of the slabs at an even rate even though the volume delivered is small.

Drip systems for rockwool slabs should deliver from .25 gallons to 1.5 gallons of solution per hour. Nutrient solution delivery can vary from 6 to 12 fluid ounces per emitter and still get relatively even distribution of nutrients. Watch the incline of slabs and check each emitter to ensure that it is flowing evenly.

Water uptake by plants is necessary both day and night. The greatest amount of water is taken in when light and heat are the most intense. Water uptake at night is much lower than during the daytime hours. High performance gardens are irrigated occasionally at night.

The volume and duration of each watering is set between 5 to 15 minutes for the average fast growing vegetable garden. Now, all that needs to be determined is how often to water.

Rockwool is easily and efficiently irrigated with a nutrient solution controlled by a timer.

A scale and microswitch properly set up, allows the rockwool to determine when it needs to be watered. A sample slab of rockwool is kept on a scale. When the weight falls below a "trigger point", the microswitch turns on the pump and the irrigation cycle begins. Similar watering sensors can be used, including a system that employs a plastic hose, wick or a funnel to catch water. The water is weighed to determine the next watering cycle.

Rule of Thumb: Irrigate when five to ten percent of the water holding capacity is removed from the slab.

Recycled nutrient solution is constantly changing. Salts build up to toxic levels as plants use selected nutrients within the solution. Constant monitoring and adjusting are required to provide the exact concentration of nutrients for optimum growth. With a non-recovery system, the excess nutrient solution drains off and is not reused. The plants get all the nutrients they need and any nutrients that are not used will simply drain off. A fresh nutrient solution is used for the next watering. Apply enough nutrient solution to get a 10 to 30 percent runoff to provide a leaching effect, flushing excess salts from the rockwool.

Water that evaporates from a slab leaves behind mineral salts that do not evaporate. The concentration of nutrients in the slab gets higher because of this evaporation. Cover the rockwool to keep evaporation to a minimum.

Timers

A timer is essential for high performance gardens. Use a timer to control a pump or solenoid valve(s) for gardens that need to be irrigated more than once a day.

Most people have a 120 volt timers somewhere around the house. The most convenient timer cycles for 24 hours and uses adjustable trippers that turn an electrical appliance on and off. These timers generally have a minimum "on" time of 30 minutes to one hour, which is too long to flood a rockwool garden. Cubes, slabs and flock normally require a maximum of 15 minute irrigation cycles for best performance. Roots start to get starved for oxygen and may die if the nutrient solution regularly floods the rockwool for more than 15 minutes.

Most digital timers sell for about $30 and have a minimum on time of 1 minute and a maximum of 23 hours.   They turn on and off up to four to six times a day. Set the timer for a minute or two longer than it takes to fill the growing bed to ensure it fills completely every time.

Mechanical short range and percentage cycle timers cost $60 or more and

A air conditioner timer, a heavy duty multi circuit timer, and a simple, versatile digital timer.

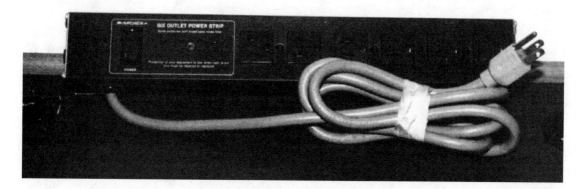

A surge protector will save pump motors and fuses from electrical fluctuations.

should be used in conjunction with a 24-hour timer. The 24-hour timer turns the short range timer "on", the short range timer cycles for one to ten minutes, then shuts off.

A   lawn sprinkler timer offers much more versatility for high performance gardens.   Naturally these timers are more expensive. These timers turn on and off for a minimum of four to twelve minutes and can cycle from 4 to 30 times every 24 hours. The control and convenience are well worth the extra expense.

Pump timers are usually 120 volts unless used for motors over 1 horsepower. surge protector saves motors and fuses from destruction.

Chapter Four

pH and Dissolved Solids

pH

PH is a scale from 1 to 14 that measures acid-to-alkaline balance. One is the most acidic, 7 is neutral and 14 is the most alkaline. Most plants will grow best in rockwool with a slab or cube pH from 5.5 to 6.5. Within this range, most plants can properly absorb and process available nutrients. If the pH is too low (acidic) the nutrients are chemically bound by acid salts and the roots are unable to absorb them. An alkaline growing medium with a high pH, will cause chemical lock-up, a possible toxic salt buildup and will limit the root's water intake.

Water that evaporates from a slab or cube, leaves behind nutrients that do not evaporate. The concentration of nutrients in a slab or cube is higher because of plant transpiration and evaporation. Roots also take nutrients up at different rates, which further compounds this nutrient concentration and imbalance.

There are several ways to measure pH. Litmus paper, liquid pH test kits or electronic pH testers may be found at most nurseries. When testing pH, take two or three samples and make sure to read and understand directions carefully before conducting the test. Use a buffer solution of known pH once a month to calibrate your measuring equipment.

Litmus paper, when compared to an electronic digital pH pen is difficult to use. Different litmus papers test different ranges of pH. Use litmus paper that tests a pH range of at least 4.5 to 6.5. Wet the litmus paper for 10 seconds with the solution to be measured. The color of the litmus paper should then be matched with a color chart. A false reading could occur if the fertilizer contains a coloring agent.

Inexpensive electronic pH meters are relatively accurate and very convenient. Easy-to-use electronic pH testers are available in garden centers and hardware stores and cost from $15 to $30. A favorite pH tester or "pH pen" retails for $50 to $60 and is very accurate. The extra investment is worthwhile if you are concerned with accuracy. These pH pens are also easy to calibrate to ensure accuracy. They should be calibrated in a buffer solution of known pH that is the same temperature as the nutrient solution.

A pH meter is actually a very sensitive voltmeter. Pure water has no resistance at all. Add an alkaline or acid fertilizer (salt) to the solution and a very faint current of electricity is produced. The meter measures this electrical current to provide a pH reading.

Higher quality meters have a temperature adjustment or compensation. The pH measurement is always sensitive to temperature. Inaccurate measurements might be recorded when the temperature is not taken into account. A stock solution kept at the same temperature as the nutrient solution to be measured with a pH of 7 is used to calibrate the pH meter. The probe(s) are placed in a pH 7 solution and a calibration screw is adjusted until the needle rests on 7. The nutrient solution can then be tested.

Checking the pH

To measure the difference in pH between the reservoir and the rockwool, nutrient solution samples should be collected from both the reservoir and the slab. A syringe can be used to extract a sample solution from the slab about two inches deep. It is the pH at the roots that is important. The pH can vary between these samples.

The results of this difference in pH between the reservoir and slab should remain relatively constant. The reservoir or input nutrient solution shows the fertilizer has been diluted correctly and is available in a soluble form for the roots. The slab or cube will show the actual pH that the roots are working in. The pH of the reservoir is generally .1 to .5 lower than the pH of the slab. If the pH climbs or drops significantly, it's time to change the nutrient solution. The change in pH could signal several different problems with nutrient balance and concentration. A pH too low or too high can make nutrients unavailable.

Take the nutrient solution sample at the same time each day in relation to the irrigation cycle so test results are consistent. Samples taken just before the irrigation cycle will show a wider spread between the pH of the input solution and the solution in the cube or slab. If you only water once a day, check the rockwool a couple of hours before and after the irrigation cycle. The readings will show the extreme highs and lows in the pH range. The pH reading after the irrigation cycle will be closer to the reservoir reading.

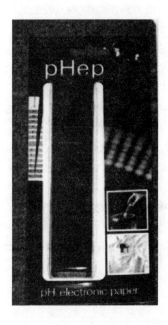
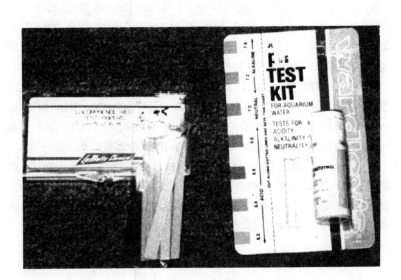

Litmus paper, a liquid pH testing kit and a pH testing pen.

Always take the cube or slab sample in the same manor and from the same location in the slab to retain consistent measurements. Use a syringe with a long nipple or a turkey baster with a   stiff hose to draw samples from the center or lower portion of the slab. You can also pick up a cube and squeeze a small amount of nutrient solution from it or if unable to pick up the cube, use a syringe,   but be very careful not to damage tender roots. It's a good idea to take samples from several different   slabs or cubes and mix all of the samples together to get an average.

Rule of Thumb: The pH of the slab and reservoir should range from 5.5 to 6.5.

Place each sample in a clean jar.   Measure each sample with the pH meter. The pH of the rockwool should be within one or two tenths of a point of the reservoir solution.

Check the pH of the water being used.   The carbonate/bicarbonate content or alkalinity of the water measures the resistance of water to acidification. If the carbonate/bicarbonate level is low, little acid is needed to lower pH and vice versa.   Rainy and coastal climates generally have acidic water, while desert regions are prone to alkaline water.

A   pH   problem may surface in the late autumn,   when leaves fall and vegetation is decomposing.   This biodegradation process may create an artificially low pH. The acidic leaves lower the pH of the outside soil and in turn lower the pH of the ground water. This problem is most common among smaller municipal water systems and well-water systems.   Larger water districts carefully monitor and correct pH so there are fewer problems for the gardener. Be on the lookout for any major environmental changes that could affect the water pH. It is important to keep an eye on the pH at all times. If the pH is within one or two tenths of a point, it is OK.

The   pH   should be checked regularly and the information recorded in a notebook or on a calendar kept near the garden. Soon you will notice patterns develop. If there is too drastic of a change in the pH you will know when to flush the system or change the nutrient solution.

A pH meter measures the pH fast and accurately.

There are several alkaline compounds that are used to raise the pH. Raising pH is usually not as necessary as lowering it.

pH Raise and pH Lower are available in both liquid and powder form.

Dilute potassium hydroxide is safe and easy to use to raise the pH. Potassium is also a necessary nutrient. Sodium hydroxide also raises pH but is very caustic and requires a mask and gloves to handle. Sodium is toxic to plants and it replaces potassium. That is, when there is an excess of sodium, plants will take up sodium rather than potassium. Sodium hydroxide will also burn skin severely in concentrated amounts.

Rule of Thumb: To raise the pH, mix a small amount of dilute potassium hydroxide per gallon of nutrient solution. Check the pH. Add small amounts of potassium hydroxide as needed.

To raise the pH use:

Rule of Thumb: To raise the pH, mix a small amount of dilute potassium hydroxide per gallon of nutrient solution. Check the pH. Add small amounts of potassium hydroxide as needed.

To raise the pH use:

Hydrated lime - slow to dissolve
Sodium hydroxide (caustic potash) - toxic
Potassium hydroxide - OK in dilute form
Calcium carbonate - insoluble
Baking soda - toxic, contains sodium
Potassium phosphate - OK, but will not do much
Dolomite lime - difficult to dissolve
Ground limestone - difficult to dissolve
Calcium chloride - is not recommended but is excellent for chlorine-loving plants like marsh grasses and artichokes.

There are many ways to lower the pH. Nitric acid works well to control pH because the nitrate supply is usually not as touchy as the phosphate supply. Commercial growers use less expensive phosphoric acid until the ppm nutrient level is met, then use nitric acid to control the balance of the pH. Calcium nitrate, phosphoric acid and sulfur compounds also work very well to lower pH. Keep a watchful eye on the pH if using fertilizers containing these nutrients, they could lower it substantially.

Many pH altering chemicals are sold at chemical supply stores in concentrated strengths. Be very careful when handling concentrated acids or alkalis. They are very caustic and can cause severe skin, eye and lung damage. Some of these chemicals are available in either liquid or powder form.

Vinegar and aspirin will also lower pH, but their effect dissipates rapidly. Only use these as a last resort or in very small gardens.

Rule of Thumb: To lower pH, add a small amount of nitric acid or calcium nitrate per gallon of nutrient solution, mix and recheck.

To lower the pH use:

Calcium carbonate - does not work well to alter pH - insoluble
Calcium nitrate - dilute solution is OK
Nitric acid - dilute solution is OK
Phosphoric acid - dilute solution is Ok
Sulfur or sulfuric acid - dilute solution is OK
Aspirin - use as a last resort and only in one gallon or less.
Vinegar - use as a last resort and only in one gallon or less.

To figure out how much chemical to apply to alter the   pH, remove a gallon of nutrient solution from the reservoir. Add half   as much   pH raise or pH lower as recommended,   then check the pH. Wait about 15   minutes, stir and recheck. When you have measured the sample and it's where you want it,   add a proportionate   amount   of   the compound to the balance   of the nutrient solution.

After altering the pH, check it, then check it again the next day after irrigating. Check the pH at least once a week to make sure it remains stable.

Conditioning

Conditioning lowers the pH of rockwool from about 8.0 to around 5.5. Conditioning also wets it thoroughly, preventing dry pockets.

To condition rockwool, fill slab's bag completely to the top with nutrient solution to ensure that it is saturated. The pH of the nutrient solution should be about 4.5 before it soaks into the rockwool. The slabs must be saturated before use.   Let the solution sit in rockwool overnight. After soaking all night,   the pH of the nutrient solution in the rockwool should be about 5.5.

NOTE: The pH of the nutrient solution will rise for the first week or two after it comes into contact with most brands of rockwool. The effect is most dynamic on new cubes, slabs and less pronounced as the rockwool's life continues. A small amount of rockwool can be boiled in distilled water and the pH measured when the water cools. If the pH is above 8.0, soak the rockwool in pH-4.0 phosphoric acid for 30 minutes and then flush. The phosphoric acid helps to neutralize the alkalinity of most brands of rockwool.

Most flowers and vegetables grow best in rockwool with a pH range from 5.5 to 6.5 and 6.0 is ideal. The pH in high performance rockwool gardens requires a vigilant eye by the gardener.   The pH of the nutrient solution can change easily. All of the nutrients are in solution within this pH range. The   roots take up nutrients at different rates. Fluctuations in the amount of nutrients in the solution will change the pH.   If the pH is not within the   acceptable hydroponic range (5.5 to 6.5), nutrients will not be absorbed as fast as possible and growth slows.

 Rule of Thumb: Check the pH regularly and make sure it is between 5.5 and 6.5.

Dissolved Solids (DS)

The total dissolved solids, also referred to as dissolved solids (DS) scale is divided up into parts per million (ppm). That is, it tells how many parts of a dissolved solid there are in a solution. A reading of 1800 ppm means there are 1800 parts of nutrient in one million parts solution or 1800/1,000,000. The dissolved solids scale is the most common. Electrical Conductivity (EC) and Conductivity Factor (CF) are also used to measure DS.

Pure distilled water has no resistance and conducts no electrical current. When some impurities are added to the pure distilled water, it conducts electricity. The elements found in the normal water supply on page 21 lists many of the impurities or dissolved solids found in household tap water. These impurities or elements conduct electricity when dissolved. Add fertilizer to the pure water and the dissolved solids (DS) climbs.

This soluble salts tester by Kelway is accurate and easy-to-use.

The   DS for most crops should stay from 1000 to 2500 ppm but in some
instances it can be as high as 3000 ppm. People have run higher on experimental
basis but it is not recommended.

The overall volume or strength of these elements may be measured with a
simple DS meter. The DS meter has two electrodes that are placed in the water
or nutrient solution. When the DS meter is switched on,   an alternating electrical
current passes between the two electrodes.   A digital display measures the
amount of current flowing between the two electrodes.   A DS reading of "0"
indicates there are no solids in the water or that the water is pure.   Pure rainwater

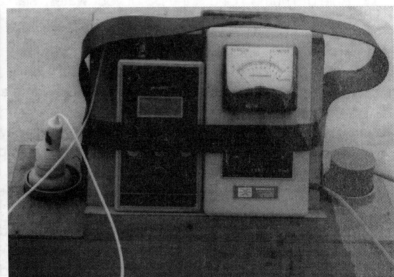

A dissolved solids pen and a very accurate set of pH and DS meters.

has an DS close to 0. If you live in the Midwest or Northeast,   be very careful when
using rainwater. The rainwater could be "acid rain." Check the DS before using.
A small amount of pH raise usually neutralizes this acidity.   Distilled water,
purchased at the grocery store, may still register a small amount of resistance as it
is not perfectly pure. Pure water with no resistance is very difficult to obtain.

Higher   quality meters have an automatic or manual temperature
adjustment. The DS measurement is sensitive to temperature. Inaccurate
measurements can be recorded when the temperature is not taken into account. A
stock solution with a DS of 1500 ppm is used to calibrate the DS meter. The
probes are placed in solution with a DS of 1500 ppm and a calibration screw is

adjusted until the needle rests on 1500 ppm. This calibration solution is to be kept at the same temperature as the nutrient solution.

A favorite meter of many hydroponic gardeners is a dissolved solids pen that costs from $50 to $60. These pens will last for 6 months to one year and are quite accurate. Pens do not have a manual temperature adjustment. Calibrate the pen with solution that is the same temperature as the nutrient solution to ensure an accurate reading.

DS measures the dissolved solids but it does not measure each nutrient. For example, a DS reading of 1500 ppm could mean there are 1000 ppm sodium and 500 ppm sulphur in solution. A DS of 1500 ppm could also measure a complete and balanced solution with all the nutrients included in the proper proportions. DS is only a valid measure when you start with the proper ratio of nutrients in solution.

 Rule of Thumb: Check the DS of your water, slab and runoff of high performance gardens regularly.

Checking the Dissolved Solids

To check the DS, collect nutrient solution samples from the reservoir and the slab or cube. Use the same principles as "Checking the pH" on page 46. Conduct both the pH and DS tests at the same time to save effort.

Place a sample from the reservoir and slab in separate clean jars. Measure each sample with the DS meter. Be careful to ensure no corrosion builds up on probes. The DS of the rockwool cubes should be equal to or up to 30 percent greater than the reservoir solution.

Under normal conditions, the DS in the slab should be 100 to 500 ppm higher than the nutrient solution in the reservoir. If more than 500 ppm, you have a salt buildup in the rockwool and should flush thoroughly with dilute nutrient solution, then replenish or change the nutrient solution.

The DS reading will rise if rockwool is under-watered or dries out. The DS may increase to two or three times as high as the input solution when too little water is applied. This increase in slab DS causes some elements to build up faster than others. For example, when the DS doubles, the amount of sodium increases four to six fold!
NOTE: there should not be any sodium present unless it is in the supply water.

To control the dissolved solid content of the nutrient solution easily, let 10 to 20 percent of the solution "run off" to waste after each watering. This "run off" will carry away any excess salt buildup.

 Rule of Thumb: to lower the DS in rockwool nutrient solution, increase runoff, flush, or change the nutrient solution.

Rule of Thumb: to raise the DS, add more fertilizer to the solution or change the nutrient solution.

A Quick Note About Fungicides and Pesticides

Take care when using pesticides and fungicides in the nutrient solution while plants are growing. Be careful about contaminating the nutrient solution with these substances. Few pesticides have been approved for rockwool and may damage sensitive roots. Use pyrethrum, *Bacillus Thruingiensis* (Dipel or Thuricide) or rotenone for pesticides and be very careful with fungicides.

Chapter Five

Cube Gardens

Rockwool cubes can be used to start seedlings or cuttings and grow small plants. They can be watered by hand from above or flooded from below. In fact, cubes even work to wick nutrient solution up to plants. As you can see, rockwool cube gardens use old established hydroponic gardening principles. Several of these established gardening principles can be combined and used with rockwool to achieve incredible yields.

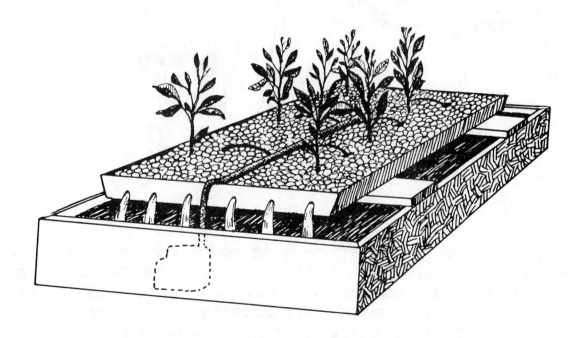

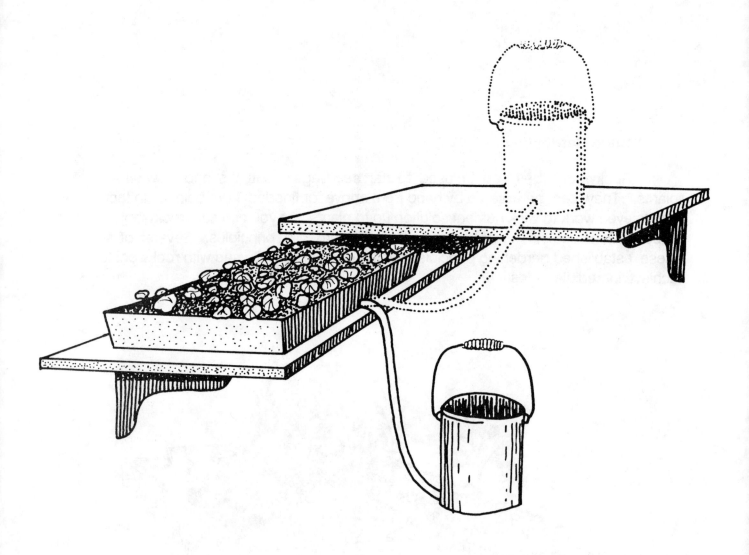

Making your own high performance ebb and flow rockwool garden is easy. The principle is simple; the nutrient solution floods into the garden bed, pushing the CO_2-rich, oxygen-poor air out. When the rockwool drains, it draws in new oxygen-rich air. A perfect environment is created for nutrient uptake and plant growth. How you employ these principles depends on how fast you want your garden to grow.

Today the flood and drain, also known as the ebb and flow method is used by many commercial hydroponic operations and many home gardens.

A small rockwool ebb and flow cube garden full of tomatoes.

The   growing   bed can be almost any size or shape as long as it holds
water.   The table should be just a little deeper than the cubes so that the cubes can
be submerged for flushing every week or two.   A growing bed or table with four-
inch sides and large,   flat ridges for drainage along the bottom is ideal for three-
inch cubes.   Many gardeners report that   complete submersion is not
necessary with cubes and grow healthy gardens using a two-inch tall sides on the
growing bed.

Rule of Thumb: Keep the roots evenly moist.

Roots must not sit in stagnant water. Water must drain freely instead of pooling or puddling up. The table should drain completely when level or set at a slight incline. Cubes can also be set on a shallow grate above the water "puddles". Rockwool that shifts into the lowest point in the growing bed will always be waterlogged unless a drain outlet is below this point. These low spots create soggy, wet conditions that promote rot and fungus. Ideally the high performance growing table bottom has broad ridges that allow the rockwool to lay flat and narrow gutters to carry away runoff. Root rot could also occur if water "puddles".

This small growing bed has groves on the bottom to carry nutrient solution back to the reservoir.

Perlite placed under the rockwool blocks allows better drainage but it's so light that it floats to one end of the table or washes down the drain. Washed gravel or expanded clay work well to create an air space below the cubes and do not wash away. The most critical point to control in a rockwool cube garden is the root zone. The root zone should stay evenly moist. The roots will die if they are drowned or dry out.

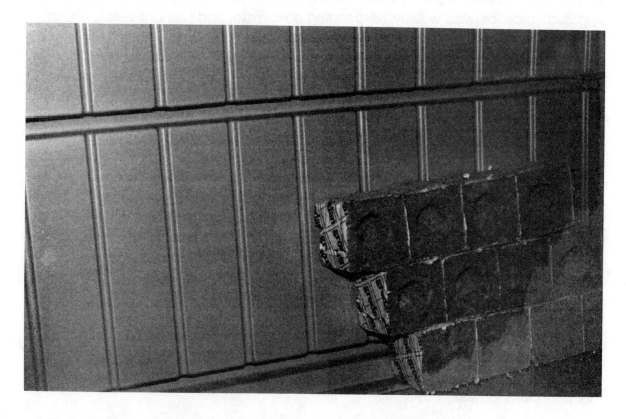

This large ebb and flow table has short sides and deep groves to channel nutrient solution

Lets look at a couple of easy-to-use window sill gardens that have no drain. We'll start seedlings in one garden and grow fresh kitchen herbs in the other. You can make a window sill seed propagation garden from 2 - 1020 nursery flats (a 1020 flat measures 10 inches by 20 inches) and a turkey baster. One flat has a lattice bottom with plenty of drain holes, the other does not.

The spring seedlings or cuttings are started in a mesh bottom flat, set inside the solid bottomed, water tight 1020 nursery flat. This garden is just like the soil seed starter kits available at many retail nurseries and mail order stores. The only difference is that this rockwool starter kit is easier and more productive than the soil kits. Once you try it, you'll love it. The solid bottomed flat serves as a reservoir. The rockwool cubes are set inside the mesh bottomed 1020 nursery flat which is the growing bed. A turkey baster, available at the supermarket, is used to draw nutrient solution from the bottom flat and apply it to the top of the rockwool cubes. The nutrient solution mix is one quarter to one half strength. Cubes are irrigated once or twice weekly, depending on climate, and size of the little plants. The rockwool cubes should stay very wet and retain good drainage. The larger root system of established seedlings will use more nutrient solution. Within a few weeks, the roots grow out the bottom of the rockwool into the nutrient solution. When the roots show through the one-inch cubes, harden-off by placing the garden outdoors in the shade for a couple of hours each day. A few days of hardening-off before transplanting into the outdoor garden will ensure vitality.

The second ebb and flow garden has a larger reservoir and takes up a little more space. To make this garden: attach a reservoir bucket to the garden bed with a flexible hose. Drill a half-inch hole in the bucket and garden bed. Insert a threaded half-inch male PVC fitting with a rubber washer through the hole. Screw a threaded, half-inch female PVC fitting with a washer on the male fitting. Then glue a two-foot piece of one-inch garden hose inside the female fitting. To irrigate, raise the bucket above the garden bed so that the nutrient solution flows into the bed. Lower the bucket after the cubes have been flooded or in about 5 minutes to let the solution drain back into the bucket. Once set up, the garden is no mess and no fuss. Just lift and lower the bucket once or twice daily. Change the nutrient solution weekly. This simple ebb and flow system grows a perfect herb garden that fits in a window sill.

Rockwool cubes, are a better value than peat pellets or starter cubes. They are half the price, easier to use and more forgiving. Larger rockwool cubes are also a good value. For example, a three-inch cube costs about $.40 and a four-inch container with no soil costs about $.30. There is no soil to spill when using cubes and they are easy to move.

Growing Tips

Use a mild nutrient solution (quarter to half strength) on small seedlings and young cuttings. The tender plants can not endure a heavy nutrient concentration.

Start seeds and cuttings in one-inch rockwool cubes. Lay small seeds on top of rockwool and insert larger seeds into the pre-drilled hole. Push rockwool over the hole so that the seed stays in contact with the rockwool to remain moist. Larger seeds, such as melon, peas and cucumbers, fit in the hole easily while smaller tomato and lettuce seeds are best started by broadcasting on top and gently pushed slightly down in the rockwool. When roots emerge from the bottom and the sides of the cubes, transplant into pre-drilled three-inch or larger cubes. To harden-off, set the entire flat or garden in the shade outdoors for several hours each day. Then, leave the garden outdoors in a cold frame or greenhouse all night when the last chance of frost is past. Transplant the rockwool cubes into the garden after they have been hardened off for several days.

NOTE: Rockwool remains so wet that damping-off (rotting where the stem and soil meet) can become a serious problem. To sidestep any problems with damping-off or fungus on young seedlings and cuttings, let the surface of the rockwool dry out between waterings.

Saturate one-inch rockwool cubes with half strength nutrient solution. Increase fertilizer to full strength after transplanting, when roots show through three-inch cubes.

Set three-inch cubes in the garden bed, and saturate with half strength nutrient solution to get them established.

Rockwool cubes are very durable, but the roots they contain are very frail; take care during transplanting. Transplant shock will result if the roots are broken off and not gently returned to the medium. After careful transplanting, cycle the nutrient solution through the garden so the roots get saturated.

Unwrapped one-inch cubes are the best size to transplant into soil. The composition of soil and rockwool is distinct and each holds water at different rates. Moisture held in the rockwool is drawn away by soil. The drier soil attracts the water held in the rockwool. The larger the cube, the more difficult transplanting will be due to this change in surface tension. But it is OK to transplant four-inch cubes if large clusters of roots are dangling from the bottom of the cube. Remember to remove the plastic sleeve before transplanting into soil. If the soil is kept moist, the danger of water loss from the rockwool will be avoided.

Transplanting a small rockwool cube into soil.

Healthy roots growing out the bottom of a cube.

To flush out built-up salt:

Top off the reservoir containing the depleted nutrient solution with water just before the weekly draining. Plug the drain port and flood the bed with this now dilute nutrient solution. The solution should completely submerge all the cubes for a minute or two before draining back into the reservoir. Do not let the dilute nutrient solution set longer than 30 minutes. If the stems stay too wet, they could dampen off or rot.

If the nutrient solution is recirculated over one week, flowers and vegetables may grow slower. Salts can build up which may retard nutrient uptake. Some water supplies contain more sodium (Na+) ions than plants can use. After a few weeks, sodium may build up in the rockwool, which can kill roots and retard plant growth. This can happen with other salts or nutrients as well, but sodium usually creates the worst problems. Stay away from sodium based nutrients which add to supply water sodium.

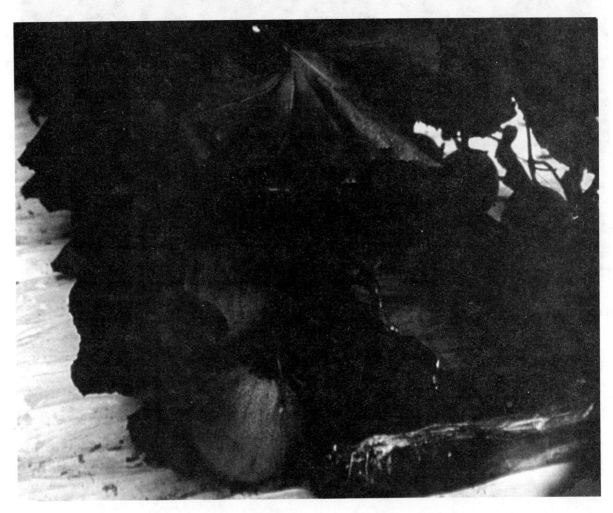

A pair of cantaloupe grown in slabs that are ready to harvest.

Even when over-watering 20 to 30 percent, there still might be a buildup of other elements. By flooding the rockwool cubes completely once a week, the ion balance will be retained. Without flooding, the upper half of the cubes may create deficiency problems.

Lattice bottomed 1020 flats are perfect containers for cubes. The open bottom adds more drainage space.

Ebb and flow technology is used extensively by commercial Dutch growers using soil and soilless mixes. These systems make the laborious chore of watering hundreds of containers with the exact supply of nutrients easy. A large table is flooded with nutrient solution then drained. Drain slots in the table channel the nutrient solution back to the reservoir or drain it to waste. The Dutch realized that it is easy to control growth while investing very little work using the flood and drain or ebb & flow tables.

American gardeners have unknowingly used Dutch ebb and flow technology for many years. Today they are at the beginning of a renaissance. Many old methods are employed to control climates with ease. Ebb and flow technology is perfect for frequent and consistent irrigation required by fast growing rockwool cubes or rockwool filled pots. All of the cubes absorb the nutrient solution at the same time. When using pots, the drain holes should be located on the sides rather than the bottom to allow better drainage.

Setting the cubes in a lattice bottomed nursery flat will keep the plants up off the bottom and trap air (oxygen) below. Just after the nutrient solution drains back into the reservoir, air bubbles can be found on the bottom of the rockwool garden bed, between the cubes and the bottom. Pick up one of the cubes and you can see air bubbles attached to the lattice below. These tiny air bubbles burst periodically releasing oxygen, to form a perfect climate for nutrient uptake.

Bob's Garden

This gardener is amazing. His name is Bob and he has found a special way to grow chrysanthemums that are at peak budding whenever desired. Bob's simple hobby turned into an obsession. He decided to control every aspect of the plants life. This method takes special advantage of all characteristics available from a small ebb and flow rockwool cube garden and more. Bob was not a gardener until he found rockwool. Now Bob grows short crops of mums with ease. He gives them away as presents for Valentines Day, Mother's Day, and assorted birthdays throughout the year. The important principles of this example must be followed to the letter for your garden to produce as well as Bob's. But do not hesitate to try new techniques or improve upon Bob's example.

Bob runs the pH at 5.5 to 6.0 and the DS at 1500 to 1800 ppm in the reservoir. He keeps the light levels at a minimum of 1000 footcandles 18 hours per day for vegetative growth and 2500 footcandles 12 hours per day for flowering growth. A maximum of 500 footcandles of light is given to cuttings.

As Bob found out, growing in rockwool is a simple matter of controlling all the factors that a plant requires to grow. Control light, air, water, nutrients, the growing medium and grow an incredible crop of mums!

Bob uses chrysanthemum cuttings to get the fastest and most consistent results.

Bob's ebb & flow garden beds are elevated so gravity will drain the solution back into the reservoir. If unable to elevate the garden bed, the nutrient solution must drain out or be pumped back up into the reservoir.

Bob's high performance ebb and flow garden uses a submersible pump and a timer. The nutrient solution is automatically recycled several times daily on 5 to 15-minute cycles. When Bob got his ebb and flow garden fine tuned, it started producing beyond his wildest dreams. He found regular monitoring and maintenance of the pH and DS are a must for the most vigorous growth. Bob uses a digital pH pen and a digital DS pen to monitor his nutrient solution. Proper pH and DS are fundamental to a perfect nutrient diet for the garden.

According to Bob, there are a few things, that when added together, make his garden so productive. It is the versatility afforded by rockwool and the simple principles listed below that function together to make Bob's garden so productive.

A quick list of these principles:

1. Since the cubes are square, they pack closer together than round pots, providing 20 percent more root growing area.

2. Even though packed tightly together, the plants are grown so short that light penetrates to the bottom leaves. And plants grow so fast, there is no time for lower leaves to yellow.

3. The roots are confined, which forces the mum's to flower a few days sooner.

4. The plants are packed so closely together that they support one another; no staking is necessary.

5. Many cuttings must be taken every few weeks. It is essential to know how long it takes for the cuttings to root, usually one to three weeks, so that they do not become rootbound.

6. The nutrient solution performs best at 70-75 degrees F 22-24 deg. C). An aquarium heater is used to maintain this temperature range in the reservoir.

7. The crop grows fast and strong before insects can set up housekeeping.

8. Artificial light, provided by a 400 watt metal halide light, attached to a timer, make total climate control possible. This garden is predicable and easier than growing outdoors! The light bill is low since the light is only on for 12 hours per day throughout the plant's life cycle. If you use natural summer light,

Bob suggests that you use a non-daylight (photoperiod) sensitive mum that will flower under 18 hours of light.

9. Its modular and versatile. A perpetual harvest is easy or you can time the harvest to be ready for somebody's birthday.

10. Higher flower to leaf ratio. Small plants yield many large flowers in relation to the volume of leaves produced.

11. The overall number, weight and size of flowers are superior using young, short plants than with large plants. It's a simple matter of counting stems.

Now we know the principles from which Bob benefits, lets look at how his garden grows.

Bob's ebb and flow table is 26 X 46 X 6 deep. The bottom of the table has small ridges but they are not tall enough to allow for perfect drainage. Bob places 21, three-inch grooved rockwool cubes in each of four 1020 lattice bottomed nursery flats. The lattice bottom, coupled with the table and ridges make a perfect root environment under the rockwool cubes. The roots stay a nice healthy fuzzy white and absorb a maximum of nutrient solution.

The 1020 flats simplify maintenance. It is easy to pick up 21, three-inch cubes, contained in a flat, all at once. In fact, Bob usually grows 21 mums for presents. When it comes time to harvest, he just removes the 1020 flat from the garden bed, sets it up on a table, squeezes the water from each of the three-inch cubes and snips the full blooming plant off at the base. Bob removes the plastic sleeve and tosses the cubes into the compost pile outdoors.

Bob changes the nutrient solution once a week to avert problems. He mixes the fertilizer into the full volume of water by sprinkling the fertilizer across the top of the water in the reservoir.

Bob transplants the cuttings into three-inch cubes when the roots show through the sides of unwrapped one-inch cubes. He waters once a day until roots show through the three-inch cube. Then he starts watering four times a day. The pump stays on just long enough to fill the garden bed about one and a half inches deep, before draining.

The fill hose for Bob's garden bed has male garden hose threads. To drain, Bob hooks up a female garden hose fitting to the male threads. Then he starts the pump and drains the reservoir out the garden hose.

Bob drains and cleans the garden every 2 or 3 months. He uses a mild bleach solution and a sponge to remove any built up algae, slime or sediments from the growing beds and holding tank.

- Mix nutrient solution A and nutrient solution B in 10 litres of water.

- When each seedling has 3 or 4 leaves, remove all but the healthiest plant from each block. Choose the two seedblocks with the healthiest plants, and insert into the mineral wool slab.

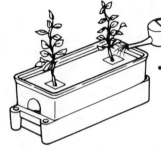

- Pour nutrient solution over slab. Ensure that the slab is well saturated. Excess solution will filter to the bottom tray. If necessary, pour contents of bottom tray over slab again.

- Excess nutrient solution will filter to the bottom tray to be wicked up as the plant requires additional water and nutrients.

- Place planter in well lighted area. In poor light conditions, artificial lighting may be necessary.

- When nutrient level falls below half, add more solution.

Courtesy Malaka Marketing Inc.
4970 Stevens Lane
Delta, B.C. V4M 1P1

Rockwool Wick Gardens

A rockwool wick garden draws the nutrient solution up from a reservoir vertically via a cube or portion of a slab tilted sideways.

Japanese - Miniponic - Nichias is the best brand of rockwool to use with wick gardens.

Capillary or wick action draws the nutrient solution to the roots. Vermiculite, sawdust, peat and soil can also be used in wick gardens. Wick gardens grow strong, healthy house plants. For rapid growing vegetables, wick gardens generally keep the medium too wet and less air is available to the roots. Wick gardens work very well if engineered properly. They have no moving parts, a low initial cost and once set up, they require little work to maintain.

Chapter Six

Slab Gardens

After seedlings get too big for the small cube garden or you have developed an insatiable appetite for fresh vegetables, a larger slab garden will bring you higher yields.

Rockwool slabs are designed for greenhouse flower and vegetable production. They will also grow a great kitchen or a patio garden. A slab will hold nutrient solution much longer than soil and will support lush growth.

To make a simple slab garden, just place a six- or eight-inch by three-inch by three-foot slab in a garden bed with good drainage. Slabs perform best in areas that provide consistent drainage such as a concrete floor, patio or greenhouse. Plastic sleeves envelop the slab to form a garden bed, a plastic grate under the slab will improve drainage. Once the slab is set in place, soak thoroughly. (See "Conditioning" page 51).

Slabs can be elevated on one end (tilted) so that gravity carries runoff back to the reservoir. Set the slabs on a flat surface that is sloping approximately two percent from end to end. A two percent slope is a drop of about one half inch from one end of a 36-inch slab to the other. Slabs set at ground level can also use gravity to deliver the nutrient solution via drip tubing.

Set the slabs up in an appropriate floor plan. Side by side or around the perimeter of a deck or patio.

Once the slabs are in position, let the water drain out by cutting two to six slits in the bottom/sides of each slab for drainage.

After the drainage holes or slits have been cut, slip one wet slab after the other into the sleeves or set into a growing bed. Make sure that there is enough sleeving at the end to channel drainage. Seal the other end of the bag off with duct tape or fold shut and secure with clothes pens. The sleeving must be dry before sealing with tape. If sleeving is unavailable, cover exposed slabs with two-ply plastic, black on the inside to stop algae growth are and white on the outside to reflect light.

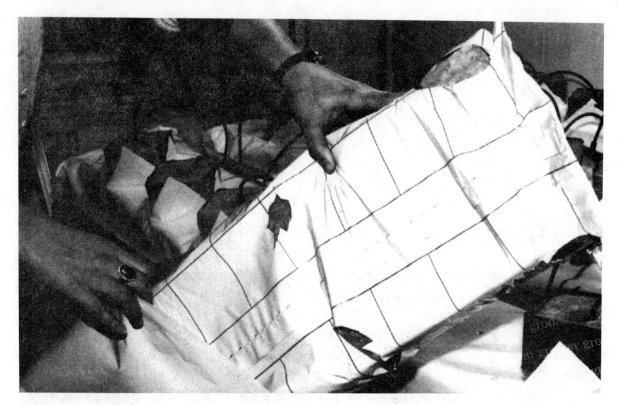

Sliding a slab into a plastic sleeve

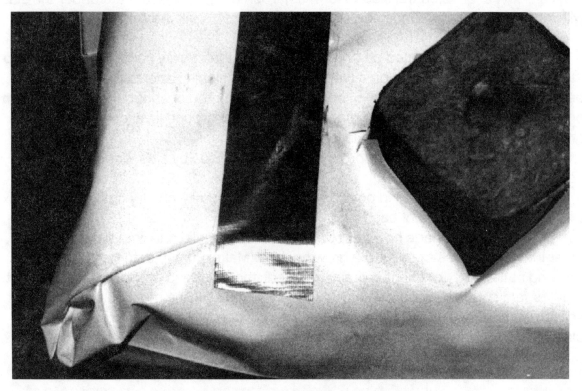

Use tape or clothes pins to seal off the end of plastic sleeves.

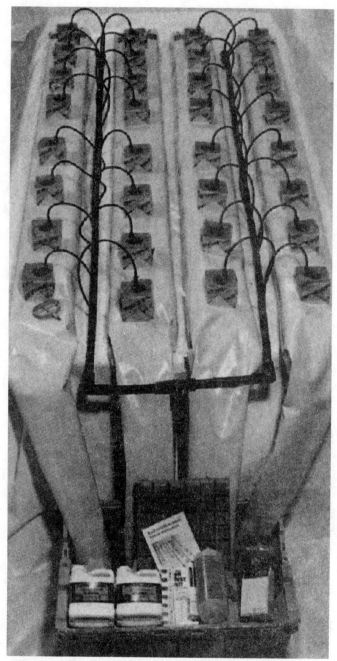

A small slab garden ready to be planted.

The sleeves are important for strong plants. Roots grow out the sides of the slabs into the moist environment between the rockwool and the plastic. This space is perfect for root growth.

To transplant, a three- or four-inch cube on to a slab, cut a hole the same size as the cube about to be transplanted in the top of the rockwool bag. The three- and four-inch cubes can be moved from the small garden and set on the slab.

Transplanting a small cube into a pre-drilled hole

Rockwool slabs are very efficient when irrigated by a drip system. Drip systems deliver the nutrient solution via a nozzle or drip emitter. The type you choose depends on your specific needs. Also see "Drip Systems" page 40.

Drip systems apply the nutrient solution to the base of each plant with a small emitter. First the emitter is placed in the cube, after one or two weeks, the dripper is placed next to the three-inch cube on the slab. This will keep the water where it is used and slows algae growth.

To set up a drip system:

Lay out half-inch drip supply tubing along side rockwool slabs and cut the tubing to length. Set stiff drip tubing in hot water to make it more pliable and easy to work with. Lay supply tubing out flat and secure in place with plastic ties or conduit tie downs. Use a hole punch, nail or electric drill to make holes in the half-inch supply tubing for the drip spaghetti tubing. The spaghetti feed tube should be long enough (12 to 24 inches) to reach each plant easily but remain out of the way. Cut the spaghetti tubing at a 45 degree angle and insert it into the hole in the half-inch tubing. Attach the other end to the drip emitter.

Secure the emitter so that it drips on the rockwool cube or slab. Take care so that the water does not run out on the plastic sleeving and spill on the floor.

One dripper should be sufficient for each plant. If one dripper does not supply enough nutrient solution to a plant,   add another dripper or use a dripper that supplies more volume.

Commercial greenhouse growers are starting to recycle the nutrient solution for conservation and ecological reasons. When no nutrient is recovered, complications and labor are reduced, but the environment may suffer if large amounts of nutrient are dumped on the ground.   Non-recovery gardens can work well for   commercial greenhouses or outdoors where runoff can be channeled away safely and efficiently. The runoff nutrient solution makes an excellent fertilizer for your outdoor garden.

For systems where the nutrient solution is recovered, make certain to change the nutrient solution every week or two. Changing the nutrient solution on the same day of the week, such as Saturday, makes it easy to remember.

To drain the reservoir,   install a "Y" in the supply hose. One end is connected to the pump and drip system and the other   to a male threaded end cap that fits a garden hose.

Cleaning and Maintenance

Flush supply lines between crops or every 2-3 months with an algacide/bactericide like Phaisan, hydrogen peroxide, bleach or potassium hydroxide (pH up). Run it through the reservoir and the supply lines. Install a valve on the end of each pipe so the solution flows through the lines and back into the reservoir. Be very careful to rinse the system with lots of fresh water to flush away the cleanser before putting the garden back into use.

Scrub out the reservoir and garden bed with a sponge and a   mild bleach solution to remove any accumulated algae or sludge.

Reusing Slabs

To reuse rockwool slabs, remove three- and four-inch cubes and discard. Remove the slab from the plastic sleeving.   When all the plastic is removed,   set the slabs up on end and turn a fan on   them so that they dry completely. Scrape any old dry roots from the sides and bottom of the slabs.

If you are concerned about virus, fungus or disease, discard slabs or steam sterilize them. A wallpaper steamer can be rented and   used to raise the temperature to 212 degrees Fahrenheit (100 deg. C) in the entire slab for 30 minutes to kill all the insects, nematodes, fungi, bacteria and viruses.

The slabs are ready to be reused after they dry out and the roots on the outside of the slabs are scraped off. Turn the slab over, bottom side up,   and insert it into a clean sleeve or set into a clean bed. Condition the slab   (page 51) then replant. Reused slabs are more prone to disease and other problems than new rockwool slabs.

Chapter Seven

Rockwool Flock

Flock is available in two forms; water repellent and water absorbent. Each of these forms is generally available in fine, medium and coarse grades.

The small bags on the left contain Grodan bags of water repellent flock and the large bag, water absorbent.

Flock or granulated rockwool is packaged in bails. Water repellent flock is available in compressed bails while water absorbent is packed in looser bails.
Water repellent rockwool is used in conjunction with peat moss or water

Insullation-grade rockwool is very economical.

absorbent rockwool to increase the air-pore space and to improve drainage.

Rockwool flock, originally manufactured as insulation, is naturally water repellent. When used as an outdoor soil amendment, it will continue to repel water for years. Unlike perlite, vermiculite or sponge rock, water repellent flock allows the root system to penetrate the fibers while adding structure to the mix.

Rockwool flock maintains its fibrous structure and air holding ability for years. The flock tilled into soil garden is easy to find two or three years later while perlite and vermiculite have long since disintegrated. Roots grow through and on the fibers so that every last bit of the flock is used.

This drawing demonstrates how rockwool flock stays in the soil to provide extra water for roots.

Rockwool flock is great for lightening clay soil. Rockwool flock is used in European soccer fields and inner cities where traffic vibrations compact soil to improve drainage.

A layer of rockwool also forms an impermeable layer for weed control plus it retains water like a sponge. One gardener laid out a three-inch layer of rockwool flock over a grass lawn. Then framed a four-foot square raised bed on top of it. Six inches of soil were added to the top of the rockwool to form the raised bed. Annual flowers were planted in the bed. The layer of rockwool underneath the garden retained so much moisture that the bed only needed to be watered half as often as other garden beds. And no grass or weeds were able to penetrate the barrier of rockwool.

Adding water repellent rockwool to heavy clay soil improves drainage substantially. The air-pore space and consequently the nutrient absorption rate increases proportionately. Compacted soils in back yards and high traffic areas also benefit from improved aeration and the soil retains the same profile.

Water repellent rockwool holds a smaller percentage of water. When mixed with the soil, water repellent flock aerates the soil. It also increases the amount of water per volume in the soil. Sound strange? Here's how it works: if one gallon of water is held by a cubic foot of soil and 25 percent rockwool is added to the soil, then there is 75 percent soil and 25 percent rockwool. Now 75 percent soil holds one gallon of water. This means that less soil holds more water. Very simple; the soil is not as dense!

A mass of roots growing from the bottom of rockwool flock

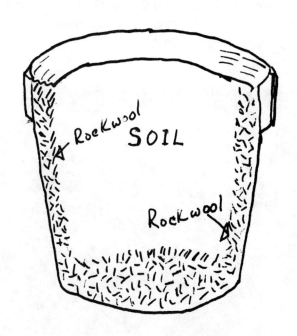

A container lined with rockwool.

Flock works great to line hanging baskets or other containers. It functions as a reservoir to hold water. Just place two or three inches of flock in the bottom of containers before filling with soil. The container will need watering about half as often as it did when it was filled only with soil. before

Custom design your own flock mix by combining water absorbent and water repellent rockwool. The exact water-holding capacity desired is easy to attain when mixing the two. The medium grade is the most commonly used in a mix and makes the most consistent medium.

Two points to consider when mixing rockwool; the water holding capacity desired and the irrigation method. Most growers start with a 70 percent water absorbent and 30 percent repellent mix. For example the fine absorbent flock holds 80 percent moisture when saturated. Add 30 percent water repellent by volume and the water holding capacity of the new mix will be about 55 percent. For house plants, the mix should contain from 5 to 30 percent water repellent rockwool. Remember slow growing house plants can tolerate more water and salt buildup than fast growing annuals. Try a few mixes, you will be surprised at the water holding and drainage provided by flock.

 Rule of Thumb: Water rockwool flock when one half of the water has been used. To test, simply weigh the container when saturated and irrigate when the plant has used half of this weight.

Orchids grow very well in rockwool flock. The rockwool flock maintains the structure and retains consistent water holding capacity and air pore space for years.

In general, fine water absorbant flock is used for propagation, medium grade water absorbant flock is best for young and medium sized plants and the coarse mix is best for mature plants. For more drainage, add 25 percent water repellent to 75 percent water absorbent mix. Work from this point to find the exact mix your plants like.

House plants grown in rockwool need fertilizer with each watering. The rockwool will hold water much longer than soil. A layer of soil or decorative rock on top will hide rockwool and stop algae growth. Rockwool can also be used in the bottom of a container to retain moisture. It works great and doesn't fall out small holes in the bottom of most containers.

Bibliography

American Greenhouse Vegetable Grower (AGVGA) Newsletters, 31 N. Market St., Elysburg, PA 17824

American Greenhouse Vegetable Grower (AGVGA) Annual Conference Proceedings, 31 N. Market St., Elysburg, PA 17824

Bridwell, R. Hydroponic Gardening. Woodbridge Press, PO Box 6189, Santa Barbara, CA 93111

Carpenter, T. 1988. Hydroponics Gardening Without Soil. Hydro-Gardens, POB 9707, Colorado Springs, Colorado 80932

Cervantes, G. 1986. Gardening Indoors: How to Grow with High Intensity Discharge Lamps. Interport, USA, Inc., P.O. Box 82009,Portland, OR 97266

Dalton, L., Smith, R. 1985. Hydroponic Gardening: Practical Guide to Growing Plants Without Soil. Cobb/Horwood Publications, P.O. Box 85-055 Sunnybrook, Auckland, New Zealand.

Douglas, J.S. 1976. Advanced Guide to Hydroponics. Pelham Books, 44 Bedford Square, London, England.

Douglas, J.S. 1984. Beginners Guide to Hydroponics. Pelham Books, 44 Bedford Square, London, England.

Greenhouse Manager Magazine, Branch-Smith Publishing, 120 St. Louis Ave., Fort Worth, TX 76104.

Growing Edge Magazine, P.O. Box 90, Corvallis, OR 97339.

Growing with Rockwool, Roger H. Thayer, 1989, Eco Enterprises, Seattle, Washington

Hydroponic Society of America (HSA): Newsletters, P.O. Box 60677, Concord, CA 94524.

Hydroponic Society of America (HSA) Annual Conference Proceedings, P.O. Box 60677, Concord, CA 94524.

International Society on Soilless Culture, Proceedings from Annual Congress, (I.S.O.S.C.) P.O. Box 52, Wagenigen, The Netherlands.

Kenyan, S. 1983. Hydroponics for the Home Gardener. Key Porter Books, 59 Front Street East, Toronto, Canada M5E1B3.

McCaskill, J. A., Plant Nutrient Facts, Hydro-Harvest, POB 4501, Hemet, CA 92343

MAFF Publications, Lion House, Alnwick, Northumberland, England NE662PF

Organic Gardening Magazine, Rodale Press, Inc., 33 E. Minor St., Emmaus, PA 18098

Resh, H.M. 1987, Hydroponic Food Production. Woodbridge Press, Box 619, Santa Barbara, CA 93111.

Smith, Dennis L. 1987. Rockwool in Horticulture. Grower Books, 50 Doughty Street, London, England WC1N2LP

Sutherland, Dr. S.K. 1986. Hydroponics for Everyone: A Practical Guide to Gardening in the 21st Century. House Publishing Pty Ltd. 10 Hyland Street, South Yarra, Melbourne, Victoria, Australia 3141

Taylor, J. 1983. Growing More Nutritious Vegetables Without Soil, Parkside Press Publishing Co., P.O. Box 11585, Santa Ana, CA 92711.

Glossary

This glossary contains many very simple and some not so simple words in the context of their usage in this book. Many examples are given to promote good indoor horticultural practices.

Absorb -- draw or take in: Rootlets absorb water and nutrients.

Acid -- a sour substance: An acidic solution has a pH below 7.

Active -- a hydroponic system that actively moves the nutrient solution

Aeration -- supplying the nutrient solution, medium and roots with air or oxygen

Aeroponics -- growing plants by misting roots suspended in air

Alkaline -- refers to medium or nutrient solution with a high pH: Any pH over 7 is considered alkaline.

All-purpose (General-purpose) fertilizer -- A balanced blend of N-P-K: all purpose fertilizer is used by most growers in the vegetative growth stage.

Annual -- a plant that normally completes its entire life cycle in one year or less: Marigolds and tomatoes are examples of annual plants.

Aphid -- small insect of various colors: Aphids suck the juices from plants.

Bacteria -- very small, one-celled organisms that have no chlorophyll.

Biodegradable -- able to decompose or break down through natural bacterial action: Substances made of organic matter are biodegradable.

Blood meal -- high-N organic fertilizer, made from dried blood:

Blossom booster -- fertilizer high in phosphorus (P) that increases flower yield.

Bone meal -- organic fertilizer high in P: Bone meal is mixed in soil to stimulate root growth of clones and seedlings.

Breathe -- Roots draw in or breathe oxygen, stomata draw in or breathe CO_2.

Bud blight -- a withering condition that attacks flower buds.

Buffer -- a substance that reduces shock and cushions against fluctuations. Many fertilizers contain buffer agents.

Burn -- 1. Leaf tips that turn dark from excess fertilizer and salt burn

Carbon dioxide (CO_2) -- a colorless, odorless, tasteless gas in the air necessary for plant life. Occurs naturally in the atmosphere at .03%

Carbohydrate -- neutral compound of carbon, hydrogen and oxygen: Sugar, starch and cellulose are carbohydrates.

Caustic -- capable of destroying, killing or eating away by chemical activity

Cell -- the base structural unit that plants are made of: Cells contain a nucleus, membrane, and chloroplasts.

Cellulose -- a complex carbohydrate that stiffens a plant: Tough stems contain stiff cellulose.

Centigrade -- a scale for measuring temperature in which 100 degrees is the boiling point of water and 0 DEG is the freezing point of water. To convert Centigrade to Farenheight: C X 1.8 + 32 = F.

Chelate -- combining nutrients in an atomic ring that is easy for plants to absorb.

Chlorophyll -- the green photosynthetic matter of plants: Chlorophyll is found in the chloroplasts of a cell.

Chlorine -- chemical used to purify water in water systems.

Chlorosis -- the condition of a sick plant with yellowing leaves due to inadequate formation of chlorophyll: Chlorosis is caused by a nutrient deficiency, usually iron or imbalanced pH.

Color tracer -- a coloring agent that is added to many commercial fertilizers so the horticulturist knows there is fertilizer in the solution. Peters has a blue color tracer.

Conditioning -- to soak new rockwool in an acidic solution to lower the pH from 8.0 to 5.5.

Copper -- one of the trace elements necessary for plant life.

Cotyledon -- seed leaves, first leaves that appear on a plant.

Cottonseed meal -- acidic organic fertilizer and soil amendment high in nitrogen.

Cross-pollinate -- pollinate two plants having different ancestry.

Cutting -- 1. growing tip cut from a parent plant for asexual propagation 2. clone 3. slip.

Damping-off -- fungus disease that attacks young seedlings and clones causing stem to rot at base: Over-watering is the main cause of damping--off.

Dissolved solids -- the amount of dissolved solids, usually fertilizer salts, that are measured in water in parts per million.

Drainage -- way to empty rockwool of excess water: with good drainage, water passes through rockwool evenly, promoting plant growth;

Drip system -- a very efficient watering system that employs a main hose with small water emitters. Water is metered out of the emitters, one drop at a time.

Fertilizer burn -- over-fertilization: First leaf tips burn (turn brown) then leaves curl.

Fish emulsion -- fish particles suspended in a liquid: Fish emulsion fertilizer is high in organic nitrogen.

Flat, nursery -- shallow (three-inch) deep container, often 10 by 20 inches with good drainage, used to start seedlings or clones.

Foliar feeding -- misting fertilizer solution which is absorbed by the foliage.

Fungicide -- a product that destroys or inhibits fungus.

Fungus -- a lower plant lacking chlorophyll which may attack green plants: Mold, rust, mildew, mushrooms and bacteria are fungi.

GPM -- Gallons per minute

Galvanized -- Zinc coated. Do not use a galvanized metal growing bed or reservoir in hydroponics.

General purpose fertilizer -- See: All Purpose Fertilizer.

Guano -- dung and remains of bats and birds, high in organic nutrients: Sea bird guano is noted for being high in nitrogen (N).

Harden-off -- to gradually acclimate a plant to a more harsh environment. A seedling must be hardened-off before planting outdoors.

Hormone -- chemical substance that controls the growth and development of a plant. Root-inducing hormones help clones root.

Hose bib -- water outlet containing an on/off valve.

Humidity, relative -- ratio between the amount of moisture in the air and the greatest amount of moisture the air could hold at the same temperature.

Hydroponics -- method of growing plants in nutrient solutions without soil.

Hygrometer -- instrument for measuring relative humidity in the atmosphere: A hygrometer will save time, frustration and money.

Inert -- chemically non-reactive: Inert growing mediums make it easy to control the chemistry of the nutrient solution.

Insecticide -- a product that kills or inhibits insects.

Iron -- one of the trace elements essential to plant life.

Jiffy 7 pellet -- compressed peat moss wrapped in an expandable plastic casing: When moistened, a Jiffy 7 pellet expands into a small pot that is used to start seeds or clones.

Leach -- dissolve or wash out soluble components of soil by heavy watering.

Leaf curl -- leaf malformation due to over-watering, over fertilization, lack of Mg, insect or fungus damage or negative tropism.

Life cycle -- a series of growth stages through which plant must pass in its natural lifetime: The stages for an annual plant are seed, seedling, vegetative and floral.

Litmus paper -- chemically sensitive paper used for testing pH.

Macro-nutrient -- one or all of the primary nutrients N-P-k or the secondary nutrients Mg and Ca.

Meristem -- tip of plant growth, branch tip.

Micro-nutrients -- also referred to as TRACE ELEMENTS, including S, Fe, Mn, B, Mb, An and Cu.

Millimeter -- thousandth of a meter; approximately .04 inch.

Moisture meter -- a fantastic electronic device that measures the exact moisture content of soil at any given point.

Necrosis -- localized death of a plant part.

Nitrogen (N) -- element essential to plant growth. One of the three major nutrients.

Non-recovery -- describes a hydroponic system that does not recover nutrient solution once applied.

Nutrient -- plant food, essential elements N-P-K, secondary and trace elements fundamental to plant life.

Organic -- made of, derived from or related to living organisms that contain a carbon molecule.

Ovule -- a plant's egg; found within the calyx, it contains all the female genes: When fertilized, an ovule will grow into a seed.

Parasite -- organism that lives on or in another host organism: Fungus is a parasite.

Passive -- describes a hydroponic system that moves the nutrient solution passively through absorption or capillary action.

Peat -- partially decomposed vegetation (usually moss) with slow decay due to extreme moisture and cold.

Perlite -- 1. sand or volcanic glass, expanded by heat, holds water and nutrients on its many irregular surfaces. 2. mineral soil amendment.

pH -- a scale from 1 to 14 that measures the acid-to-alkaline balance a growing medium (or anything): In general plants grow best in a range of 6 to 6.8 pH.

pH tester -- electronic instrument or chemical used to find where soil or water is on the pH scale.

Phosphorus (P) -- one of the three macro-nutrients that promote root and flower growth.

Photoperiod -- the relationship between the length of light and dark in a 24-hour period.

Photosynthesis -- the building of chemical compounds (carbohydrates) from light energy, water and CO_2.

Phototropism -- the specific movement of a plant part toward a light source.

Potassium (K) -- one of the three macro-nutrients necessary for plant life.

Primary nutrients -- N-P-K.

Propagate -- 1. Sexual - produce a seed by breeding a male and a female plant 2. Asexual - to produce a plant by cloning.

Prune -- alter the shape and growth pattern of a plant by cutting stems and shoots.

Pumice -- lightweight volcanic rock, full of air and water-holding cavities: Pumice is a mineral soil amendment.

PVC pipe -- plastic (polyvinyl chloride) pipe that is easy to work with, readily available and used to pipe water into a grow room or make a watering wand.

Pyrethrum -- natural insecticide made from the blossoms of various chrysanthemums: Raids' Pyrethrum is the most effective natural spider mite exterminator.

Recovery -- a recovery hydroponic system recovers the nutrient solution and recycles it.

Root -- 1. the tender light- and air-sensitive underground part of a plant: Roots function to absorb water and nutrients as well as anchor a plant in the ground. 2. to root a cutting or clone.

Root hormone -- root-inducing substance.

Safer's Insecticidal Soap -- Insecticidal soap: Controls just about all bad insects including the hated and feared SPIDER MITE.

Salt -- crystalline compound that results from improper pH or toxic buildup of fertilizer. Salt will burn plants, preventing them from absorbing nutrients.

Sand -- heavy hydroponic soilless medium amendment: Coarse sand is excellent for rooting cuttings.

Secondary nutrients -- calcium (Ca) and magnesium (Mg).

Seed -- the mature, fertilized, ovule of a pistillate plant, containing a protective shell, embryo and supply of food: A seed will germinate and grow, given heat and moisture.

Soluble -- able to be dissolved in water.

Sphagnum moss -- moss grown in Canada, used for soil amendment and hydroponic soilless medium.

Square feet (sq. ft.) -- length (in feet) times width equals square feet.

Starch -- complex carbohydrate: Starch is manufactured and stored food.

Sterilize -- make sterile (super-clean) by removing dirt, germs and bacteria.

Stress -- a physical or chemical factor that causes extra exertion by plants: A stressed plant will not grow as well as a non--stressed plant.

Stomata -- small mouth-like or nose-like openings (pores) on leaf underside, responsible for transpiration and many other life functions: The millions of stomata, must be kept very clean to function properly.

Sulfur -- one of the trace elements essential to plant life.

Sugar -- food product of a plant.

Super-bloom -- a common name for fertilizer high in phosphorus (P) that promotes flower formation and growth

Synthesis -- production of a substance, such as chlorophyll, by uniting light energy and elements or chemical compounds.

Sump -- reservoir or receptacle that serves as a drain or holder for hydroponic nutrient solutions.

Tap root -- the main or primary root that grows from the seed: Lateral roots will branch off the tap root.

Teflon tape -- tape that is extremely useful to help seal of pipe joints.

Terminal bud -- bud at the growing end of the main stem.

Thermostat -- a device for regulating temperature: A thermostat may control a heater, furnace or vent fan.

Toxic life -- the amount of time a pesticide or fungicide remains active or live.

Transpire -- give off water vapor and by products via the stomata.

Trellis -- frame of small boards (lattice) that trains or supports plants.

Vermiculite -- mica processed and expanded by heat. Vermiculite is a good soil amendment and medium for rooting cuttings.

Vitamin B$_1$ -- Vitamin that is absorbed by tender root hairs, easing transplant wilt and shock.

Wetting agent -- compound that reduces the droplet size and lowers the surface tension of the water, making it wetter. Liquid concentrate dish soap is a good wetting agent if it is biodegradable.

Wick -- part of a passive hydroponic system using a wick suspended in the nutrient solution, the nutrients pass up the wick and are absorbed by the medium and roots.

Wire ties -- Paper-coated wire ties are excellent for tying down or training plants.

Zinc -- an essential trace element.

Index

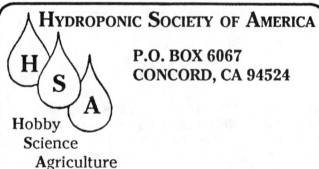

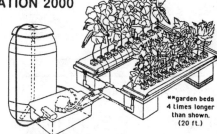

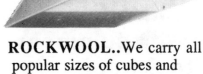

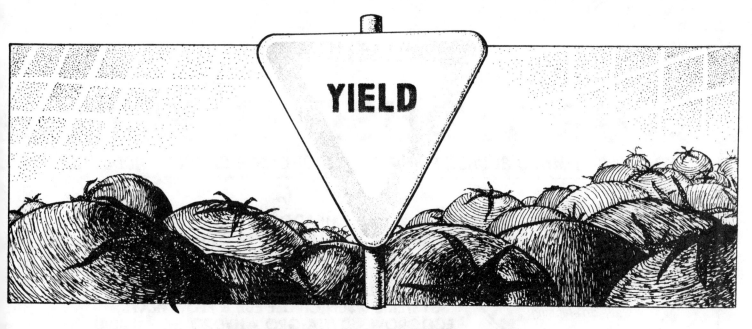

BIG YIELD
(NO PROBLEM)

It takes work; attention to details, positioning plants, maintaining temperature and humidity, trellising, pruning, training and general good housekeeping.

It takes know how; hands on, indoor gardening experience, resources for superior technology and high yield techniques, and an ear for other growers' experiences and practical solutions to common problems.

For a decade we've shared our experience and sold to serious gardeners, the equipment and supplies we know to be the best. We're dedicated to offering a variety of high quality systems and supplies and creating those that aren't available.

HIGHLIGHTS

- A full line of heat and humidity sensors, controls and exhausts for indoor and green house gardens.

- Pumps, timers, reservoirs, fittings and more for the do-it-yourselfer.

- Latest, and best performing H.I.D. lamps, ballasts, and reflectors.

- The very best hydroponic nutrients and soil fertilizers

New Product
We are now able to offer the first of our own Dutch Majic line of nutrients. These products are being developed to give growers "system-specific" compounds. System-specific because every system puts unique demands on the nutrients that are meant to feed the plants. Demands that can defeat the "one-size-fits-all" nutrients now dominating the market and keeping your plants from their full potential.

We've used the latest Dutch technology from the Naaldwijk Research Center along with information from top indoor gardeners to formulate a fully chelated nutrient compound specifically for recirculating Rock Wool Systems.

DUTCH MAJIC
NUTRIENTS ®

Dealer inquires welcome

future garden supply inc.

©1990 Future Garden Supply Inc.

12605 Pacific Avenue, Tacoma, WA 98444
Tech Line 206-531-9641   Order Line 1-800-237-6672

Grow & Tell

Once you see how easy it is to create a bountiful indoor garden you'll want to tell everyone how successful they can be with New Earth!

Our wide variety of quality gardening products will help you make your garden more productive than ever. We stock only products that are tried and true and have lots of the brand names you know and trust. Names like Diamond Lights, Green Air, Aquaculture, Hydrofarm, and General Hydroponics, just to name a few. That is why you will feel confident when you choose from our huge selection of hydroponic supplies, lights, fertilizers, propagation products, rockwool, timers, atmosphere controls, CO_2 systems, natural insect controls and books.

Got a question? We have first-hand experience with all of our hydroponic gardens and over 20 years of indoor gardening expertise. Our answers will be accurate and knowledgeable because your success is our number one priority!

Make the green thumb difference—the New Earth way!

Business hours: Tuesday through Saturday, 10–6. MasterCard & VISA accepted. Call or write for a free catalog.

NEW EARTH
INDOOR/OUTDOOR GARDEN CENTER
4422 East Highway 44 • Shepherdsville, Kentucky 40165

Give us a call at 1-502-543-5933 or toll-free at

1-800-462-5953

Stop by our grow rooms for a hydroponic taste treat.

We don't think one size fits all.

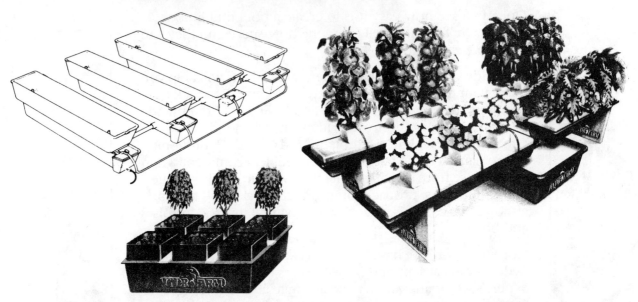

Let us help find the right system for you.

We offer hydroponic and organic garden supplies with the knowledge, customer support and experience to back them up. You may choose over 350 products from manufacturers such as Applied Hydroponics, Aqua Culture, Sun Circle, General Hydroponics, GrowMaster, and a host of others. We can offer you packaged systems to meet the most demanding need, or help you custom tailor the system that is perfect for you. Stop in any Worm's Way store and see hydroponics in action!

Growing *EDGE* subscriptions & back issues:

☐ **U.S. Orders: (3rd Class Mail)**
I have enclosed $19.95* for one year
(4 issues)of **The Growing *EDGE***
start with Vol. 2#2

☐ **U. S. Orders: (1st Class Mail)**
I have enclosed $24.95* for one year
(4 issues) of **The Growing *EDGE***
start with Vol. 2#2

☐ **Canadian Orders** (1st Class Mail):
I have enclosed $24.95* for one year
(4 issues) to **The Growing *EDGE***
start with Vol. 2#2

Back Issues of The Growing *EDGE*:

☐ Vol. 1 #1—$6.50:

Hydroponics—The Growing Technology of the 1990's
Back to the Future? Organics in Hyroponics
Hard Rock Gardening—Keeping Up with the Rockwool
   Revolution
The Fungal Underground—Mycorrhizal Associations
   and Plant Growth
The Basics of HID Lighting for the Home Gardener
Valley of the Shadow—Lighting Your Way to Mental
   and Physical Health
Nutrient Management Techniques
Winter Grown Tomatoes from North of the Border
Environmental Dynamics in the Grow Room—Part One
Oyster Mushrooms—Growing Your Own

☐ Vol. 1 #2—$6.50:

Commercial Basil Production for the Small-Time Operator
Propagation in Rockwool—Cubes, Clones and Cuttings
Biological Pest Control—The New Bottom Line
Tissue Culture—The Fine Art of Micropropagation
The Chemical Dynamics of Hydroponic Nutrient Solutions
Phytofarms of America—Assembly Line Herbs and Vegetables
You Are What Your Plants Eat—Toxics in the Garden
Environmental Dynamics in the Grow Room —Part Two
Gardening With Mushrooms—Wine-Red Stropharia

THE GROWINGEDGE
P.O. Box 1027
Corvallis, OR • 97339
(503) 757-0027 • **FAX** (503) 757-0028

☐ Vol. 1 #3—$6.50:

Bananas: Grown in Oregon
Retail Farming: In-Store Hydroponics in Houston
Integrated Pest Management for the Home Gardener
Hydroponic IPM
Bioponics: Organic Hydroponic Gardening
Hydroponics for the Home Hobbyist
Qubec's Hydroponic Tomatoes: An Alternative
   to European Imports
Exotic Mushroom Cultivation at Home—Shiitake
Root Death: Causes and Treatments
   in Reciculating Systems
Plus Regular Departments like News Clips,
   Exchange and The Cottage Cultivator

☐ Vol. 1 #4—$6.50:

Build Your Own Hydroponic System!
Know Your Software—Plant Selection for the Hydroponic
   and Greenhouse Grower
Water Should Taste Good—to Plants!
Mid-South Greenhouse and Produce
Canola Competition
Basil Production for the Small-Time Operator—An Update
Look Out Holland, Here Comes B.C.!
House Breaking Mushrooms—Grow Your Own Indoors
Softwood Cloning for Beginners
Plus Regular Departments like News Clips, Exchange
   and The Cottage Cultivator

Rockwool doesn't grow plants...

...Nutrients do!

The best nutrients produce the best results!

To achieve the fastest growth and highest yields you have to use the best nutrients. We proudly present our "ADVANCED NUTRIENT SYSTEM" which is a revolutionary combination of mineral nutrients and state-of-the-art chelates. Plus a unique pH buffering system offering the rockwool user advantages no other nutrients can. Our exceptional "Building-block" technique enables the grower to customize special formulas for many different types of plants. You can also adjust for each different phase of growth, for seedlings, to vegetative, to flowering and to fruit production. Other custom blends such as special formulas for starting cuttings and even seeds are possible. Contact us for additional information and for a supplier in your area.

GENERAL HYDROPONICS

50 Belvedere Street, Suite C, San Rafael, California 94901-4817. Telephone (415) 457-1041

Order Form

Telephone orders: Call **1-503-775-3815**

Postal Orders: Van Patten Publishing
                     4204 S.E. Ogden, Suite 201
                     Portland, OR 97206

Please send the following books. I understand that I may return any books for a full refund within 30 days of purchase, regardless of the reason, with no questions asked.

_____

_____

_____

_____

Please add my name to Van Patten Publishing's mailing list so that I may receive information on new books as they become available.

Name:_____

Address:_____

City: _____ State:_____ Zip:_____

Gardening: The Rockwool Book: $14.95 + $3.00 = $17.95
Organic Garden Basics: 12.95 + 3.00 = 15.95
Organic Garden Vegetables: 9.95 + 3.00 = 12.95

Shipping: Please include $3.00 per book for postage, handling and insurance.

Please make checks payable to Van Patten Publishing.

Order Today!

New from Van Patten Publishing

Organic Garden Vegetables

This book is packed with exact information that gives all gardeners quick answers to difficult problems. Whether you are a beginner or an expert, the easy-to-use format puts precise details at your fingertips in seconds.

Easy-to-reference facts on climate, soil preparation, planting, crop care, harvesting, kitchen ideas and exact details on growing over 300 varieties of vegetables.

A complete practical guide to over 500 diseases, insects and problems that affect vegetables. The easy-to-read style makes this book a quick, easy reference you'll be turning to for years.

Organic Garden Vegetables

Easy, complete, "how to" guide on growing over 70 herbs and vegetables without chemicals. Everything you need to know to grow vegetables organically is in this book.

George F. Van Patten

Organic Garden Basics

Easy, complete, "how to" guide on chemical free gardening, packed full of drawings, examples and expert advice on everything you need to garden organically.

George F. Van Patten

Organic Garden Basics

Every year home gardeners dump ten times more chemicals on their gardens than commercial farmers. These toxic substances contaminate ground water and pollute the environment, threatening our existence. With just a little care and management this problem can be avoided.

This comprehensive, practical manual is packed full of basic "how to" examples that make organic gardening fun, simple, safe and easy. Beginners and experts alike will find countless handy, time saving answers and ideas in this easy-to-use guide.

How to build soil, compost, fertilize, conserve water, stop weeds, buy seeds and plants, grow flowers, vegetables, shrubs and trees, natural pest control, container gardens, garden gear and much more are included in this complete handbook.

About the author:

George F. Van Patten puts more than twenty years of gardening experience at your fingertips with this series of organic garden books. His expert advise has helped thousands of gardeners turn simple, yet effective organic gardening techniques into bountiful landscapes. He has owned and operated landscape businesses and a retail garden center which gives him the hands on experience necessary to explain exactly what you need to know to grow the best garden possible. He resides in Oregon where he continues to write and maintain a delightful suburban organic garden.